Edmund Harold is a well known lecturer and for some thirty years has been a practitioner of natural healing therapies, first in England where he was born, and latterly in Australia where he now resides. He is also the founder of organisations such as The Spiritual Venturers Association and The Bridge to Christ Consciousness, both of which devote their energies to the furtherance of spiritual awareness worldwide.

Edmund lectures widely - in New Zealand, England, Austria, Switzerland, Canada, South Africa and Australia. His current project is the establishment of a centre in northern New South Wales, where he will focus on training others to develop and express their latent spiritual qualities. He is the author of *Healing for the Aquarian Age*, *Vision Tomorrow*, *Master Your Vibration*, *Crystal Healing* and *Know Yourself - Heal Yourself*

S E C O N D SIGHT
Developing The Art of
MEDIUMSHIP

Grail

Publications

Grail Publications,
P. O. Box 2316, Port Macquarie, NSW 2444.. Australia.

First published by Grail Publications 1994

ISBN 0 646 16649 2

Produced by Grail Publications,
P. O. Box 2316, Port Macquarie, NSW 2444. Australia.

 Typeset in Palatino Font 9: 12:

Printed by McPhersons Printing Group,
Suite 105, 83 Longueville Road,
Lane Cove, NSW 2066.

Contents

Illustrations

PREFACE

On looking back over my life, I now realise that I could not have taken any other path through life than the one I have followed for the past thirty years. Despite this, the role of the seer was always unwelcome, and the thought of becoming a trance channel I cared for even less. My early rejection of these tasks was largely due to ignorance of my personal destiny, and a definite fear of the unknown. Many people are quite astonished by this statement, given the measure of assistance I have received since I was quite a small boy, but I must state that none of that activity took place with my conscious permission.

A highly sensitive child, constantly experiencing out of body experiences which I could not control and which no-one could explain, I responded fearfully. There were many times as a child, when I felt like the Michelin Man, with parts of my body greatly enlarged, yet the remainder stayed quite normal. As all of this took place in the dark, as I sought to sleep, I began to fear the night. It was not until many years later, as I consciously began to develop my trance potential, that I found the answer. As I began to emerge from my physical form, this sensation of growing larger and larger was repeated.

The fears of my childhood were then laid to rest.

At the ripe old age of twenty-four, I finally discovered just what my life's purpose was. This gave me tremendous impetus and helped me, in a measure, to accept my spiritual talents. However, I had deliberately blocked these when I reached puberty. In common with everyone else, I must slowly and laboriously reactivate my clairvoyant ability.

To this end, my Spirit Mentor (or teacher) Wen Shu, who had inspired me throughout childhood, suggested one day that I book a holiday in a remote area of Cornwall, in the West of England, and be prepared to meditate daily. I happily agreed with the idea of the holiday although I had definite ideas about meditation. Once there however, the Brothers of the Light - a group of spirit teachers who, together with Wen Shu, had for some years sought to widen my spiritual horizon-determinedly began to instruct me in the art of seership, and in particular, the meaning of symbols.

They showed me the image of a cockerell, which I gazed at uncomprehendingly. Patiently, Wen Shu asked, "Well, my son, what do you see?" Shrugging my shoulders I responded "A cockerell!" "And what is its meaning?" he probed. "I haven't a clue." I replied, quite bored by this experience, my eyes fixed on the sun streaming in through the windows and the long golden beach below.

"Then pay attention and endeavour to translate the symbol my son," he persisted. "What does a cockerell do?" "Oh, it wakes people up" I said rather crossly. Ignoring my petulance, he continued,

"Then translate the symbol for me. What would this imply if it were were given to you on behalf of another person?" Realising that I would get no peace unless I co-operated I pondered on the symbol. "I suppose it means that this person must go out into the world and wake people up" I said eventually. "Awaken them to what my son? Think carefully. . . " This threw me into confusion, for I had expected him to provide the answer. "Well, a cockerell awakens people to a new day so... I suppose it means to awaken people to a new age?" I said hopefully. "Correct my son" he replied, beaming at me in his loving way.

Thinking that the lesson was over for the day I rose only to be told that I must remain indoors and continue. "Oh, but I cannot be bothered, I wish to go out and along the beach. . ." the reply to this was the image of a donkey. So, very reluctantly, I continued throughout that week the task of reactivating my seership potential. In the process I somehow tapped into my subconsious memory, bringing to light all manner of knowledge relating to the meaning of symbols.

In this manner I reluctantly became a channel. But I admit I was not always constant for on several occaisions and for different reasons, I abandoned the role, fulfilling my destiny in other ways. Always extremely patient, the Brothers permitted me to resolve my inner conflicts alone and unaided and finally, I chose to accept the mantle of the seer. It was some years before I received some feedback on just how the inspiration I had shared with others had changed their lives, enabling some among them, to develop their own skills and to go out and serve mankind.

The information which I share in these pages has been tried and tested over many years, and I offer it in the hope that those who study it will put it to good use. Those who desire to become the symbolic 'Messengers of the Gods' once more, must always endeavour to stretch themselves daily. And above all, instruct those who are drawn to them in their hour of need, on just what the purpose of *their* life is.!!

Acknowledgements

Although this book reflects my spiritual journey through this current lifetime, there are certain people who have made this a worthwhile journey and whose loving labour have made this book readable.

To Leona Lal Singh I extend my grateful thanks for her beautiful illustrations and for her wonderful cover design. There is old saying is that 'you can never tell a book by its cover' but in this instanceI feel that Leona has captured perfectly, the substance of the book.

To Patricia Mary Walker I shall be eternally grateful. At a difficult time in her own life she took the time to cast her practiced eye over my manuscript and patiently edited it - making many constructive suggestions.

Over the years, Wen Shu and the Brothers of the Light patiently, and with great forbearance, taught me my craft, instructing me daily in the art of seership despite my extreme reluctance - and Leonine stubborness. To them I owe all, for without their invaluable assistance, I could not have reached this point upon my life's path.

SECOND SIGHT

Developing The Art of

MEDIUMSHIP

EDMUND HAROLD

Illustrated by
Leona Lal Singh

Published by Grail Publications.
P. O. Box 2316, Port Macquarrie, NSW 2444
Australia.

CHAPTER 1

SECOND SIGHT

This physical realm wherein we currently have our being is a dense and illusionary environment within which the human race gathers all manner of necessary experience, each individual in turn absorbing lessons from situations and opportunities they meet during the course of daily life.

By and large, we tend to respond to everyday events in this three-dimensional world through the five lower (or physical) senses, touching and smelling many of the delightful or unusual things we encounter during the course of day to day events. In addition we also hear all manner of sounds, ranging from birdsong to stimulating music and most of humanity is able to taste the fruits of the earth and see its many wonders.

Yet few among us are aware of the higher planes of consciousness and the spiritual senses we all possess by right. In fact the vast majority of mankind feel no urge to go beyond the boundaries defined by the physical senses or to investigate the great unknown. For most appear to be fairly content with their lot in life within this material realm.

However, we must not lose sight of the fact that we are in essence Spirit Beings, temporarily visiting this Plane of Matter. Whilst clad in earthly form and surrounded by the ever present illusions of this three dimensional world, most of us tend to over-look the whole purpose of the current incarnation, undertaken in a bid to attain a greater degree of self-mastery.

The Soul - a timeless being which is the reincarnat-ing entity - also possesses sensory abilities and these higher senses, once activated, enable those who so desire, to discover entirely new dimensions and to communicate with ease with those who dwell there.

These higher senses are called 'clairvoyance' (the ability to 'see' and 'clairaudience' the capacity to 'hear' that which is said upon those same planes.

These are qualities possessed by all, yet few care to acknowledge or to activate them, often due to a fear of the unknown or simply because of the pressure which is often brought to bear upon them by those who are, in themselves, quite ignorant of the true pattern of the evolutionary process of the soul.

Sadly, the human race tends to fear what it does not understand and in the past, many gifted individuals were attacked or put to death for daring to express that to which they were made privy to on the inner level.

For instance, The Maid of Orleans - Jean d'Arc, was burnt at the stake as a heretic during the fifteenth century. Many others met a similar fate when denounced as witches. Most of course were but simple people gifted with the ability to observe the nonphysical realms, and to receive inspiration from on high.

The information contained in this book has been set down in a bid to cast the light of truth on some old phobias; to illustrate some of the pitfalls which occur along the way, and in general, to present the seeker after truth with a practical approach to the whole field of mediumship.

I have had to face and then conquer irrational fears which can beset all who seek to extend their level of consciousness beyond that which is considered to be the 'norm'. Subsequently I discovered for myself the great joy that comes with the knowledge that life is truly a continuing experience. Furthermore, having received much loving support from the Brothers Of The Light over many years, I personally encourage each of you in turn to determine to reach out beyond your personal limitations and to go out and discover your *true* self. . . Bon voyage.

CHAPTER 2

ORACLES PROPHETS AND SEERS.

Throughout the history of the human race there have been many references to gifted individuals, each of whom served the people of their time, utilising gifts or 'talents of the spirit', qualities which set them apart from all others. The memory of their attainments still lingers, and despite statements made by some sceptics today, many people feel an affinity with seers and prophets of the past and long to emulate them.

Mention Merlin the Enchanter and many people become interested, his name striking a chord deep within. Others may feel a deep affinity with the the French mystic Nostradamus, or a strong pull toward the Oracle of Delphi. We must ask ourselves, is this simply a matter of curiousity or have we in fact encountered these people or their teachings at another point in time?

Who are these mysterious individuals who appear from time, make their mark upon humanity and then vanish leaving the human race puzzled and, anxious about the future?

They are of course those who are known as the *'bearers of light'* . These 'gifted ones' who make their appearance upon this planet when our civilisations become corrupt or the race loses its sense of direction. They are sent by Greater Minds in a bid to stimulate true thought and action within humanity.

The Old Testament is replete with references to the prophets, such as Isaiah, Daniel and Zachariah, to name but a few. This is a clear indication that a Greater Mind perceives the need to provide the human race with positive leadership or direction at times of great confusion.

These mysterious beings reappear in different guises from age to age, for The Master Jesus of Nazareth is quoted as saying to the disciples, "Who is it that they say that I am? Is it not that I am Isaiah who was to come? Yet Isaiah came and they knew him not..." The disciples then realised that He spoke to them of the Baptist.

An Oracle was a priest or priestess who made prophetic anouncements at the shrine of a god and the ancient world had many oracles. By far the most famous of these was the Oracle of Delphi, located within the Temple of Apollo. According to ancient myths, Apollo himself originally made an annual prophecy through the oracle, who was referred to as The Pythia.

This was a woman of mature years who left her family and dedicated her life to the god. Prior to the act of channelling, the Pythia would purify herself at one spring on the sacred site, before drinking from a second. She was then bound and positioned adjacent to a fissure within the earth from which flowed noxious gasses and fumes. These, coupled with the laurel leaves she was first expected to chew, rendered her partly unconscious and she eventually began to speak in strange languages, or make garbled and incoherant statements, which were then translated by the priests of that temple.

Much later, this practice was amended and the oracle was placed upon a huge tripod, known as the Chair of Apollo, which was positioned directly above the earth vent, around which the temple had been constructed. The oracle was always hidden from view in the inner sanctum and those wishing to obtain direction would first pay the priests, before shouting out the nature of their enquiry.

As the Oracle gained in popularity, the prophecies were increased to one per month for the nine months of the year that the god was in residence within the sanctuary. The prophecies always took place on the seventh day of the month (seven being *the* occult number). There were of course a great many channels or oracles over the centuries - it was not simply a case of one talented individual. In fact hundreds of gifted women kept this tradition alive at Delphi for many centuries

The most famous prognostication attributed to the Oracle was on behalf of Croesus, King of Lydia, Lydia, who was incredibly wealthy. He was greatly concerned as to the true intent of his neighbour, the King of Persia and desired to locate a true oracle. He sent messengers to all the oracles then functioning in the ancient world, but only the Oracle of Delphi correctly answered the question he placed.

Overjoyed, he sent her great gifts, which subsequently led to the many stories about the wealth of the of the Oracle. He then asked her whether he would be successful in defeating the Persians but alas he failed to correctly interpret her answer. The Oracle told him that if he marched against the Persians a great empire would be destroyed. Greatly encouraged by this Croesus attacked and lost his kingdom. The Oracle had been correct once again.

The tales which abound with regard to King Arthur and his Knights of the Round Table, coupled with those about Merlin the Enchanter, are invariably dismissed as mere myths, as indeed many of them are. However Arthur and Merlin did exist, Arthur being a celtic warrior circa 500 AD. Those were turbulent times for England and a great warrior had to be found who could lead the people towards a more civilised way of life.

The being whom we refer to as Merlin was one of those advanced souls who make their appearance when mankind requires powerful direction and the life as Merlin, was in fact an early incarnation of the Ascended Master Ragoczy. He purposefully created a situation which would lead to the birth of Arthur - whom we know today as the Ascended Master Kut-Humi.

The Knights of The Round Table were established by Merlin as a chivalrous order, and the knights

The Ascended Master Ragoczy

Once known to mankind as Merlin the Enchanter, this Illumined One has influenced the human race throughout recorded history, appearing as Francis Bacon, at the court of Queen Elizabeth the First of England, and more recently, as the Comte de St Germain, a confidante of King Louis the XV1 of France, and his Queen, Marie Antoinette.

The Ascended Master Kut Humi

This Master Soul is the Co-Protector of The Grail, together with the Arch-Angel Michael, and has inspired the human race at various points during its evolution incarnating as King Athur, during the 6th Century AD: Pythagorus, the Greek philosopher of the 6th century BC - known as the Father of modern mathematics and in the 12th century AD when he appeared as Francis of Assisi.

themselves were all Grade Three Initiates of the of the Greater Mysteries. Indeed, all of the tales we read in childhood about the knights, were in fact stories of their many initiations all undertaken in a bid to locate and attain the mythical Grail. This fabled cup of light represents the eternal search for truth for which some determined souls continue to search, life after life.

We now know Merlin as The Ascended Master Ragoczy and He still seeks to guide those who, in the past, were impressed to take up the search for truth and undergo a series of difficult initiations or cleansing situations. Those who today feel a deep deep affinity for this advanced soul are among a body of individuals who are once more being called to take up the cause anew and possibly, to play their part in the spreading of the light of truth.

In recent years the prophecies of Nostradamus have begun to make a great impact upon twentieth century thinking as it becomes evident to most rational thinkers that many of the prophecies made by this great seer in the sixteenth century have since come to pass.

He was able to forsee events that he could not begin to imagine such as the dawning of the French Empire whose Emperor he stated would be born close to Italy. This prediction related to Napoleon Bonaparte who was born on the island of Corsica. But during the sixteenth century, France was ruled by kings, and the concept of a great empire led by a mighty emperor must have appeared quite improbable. Nostradamus also predicted the rise to power of Adolph Hitler whom he referred to as Hister.

He lived during the time of the dreaded inquisition and was forced to flee as news of his prophetic ability spread. He also made several prophecies relating to the royal family of that period and in an uncanny manner predicted precisely the manner in which the King, Henry the Second, would meet his end; ie in a joust with a fatal wound to the eye.

Nostradamus set his predictions down as four line poems or quatrains and in a bid to deflect possible in vestigation it is said that he threw his predictions in the air and collated them in the order in which they fell. This act of self preservation has led to much controversy throughout the centuries with many people today still seek to find their true meaning, and the events they predict.

This gifted seer practised scrying. This art involved using a bowl of water, the surface of which was illuminated by the flame of a candle. This provided him with a mirror-like surface which served to reflect his clairvoyant faculty. In this manner he was able to forsee the sailing of the Spanish Armada, and its subsequent defeat by the English fleet; the development of atomic weapons and their use during the second World War.

The twentieth century has also produced its share of seers, the most widely recorded being Edgar Cayce, known as the 'Sleeping Prophet'. Edgar Cayce had the ability to go into a self-induced trance-like state and project his consciousness to different cities and towns all over the United States of America. In this 'out of body' state he made medical diagnosis on behalf of some thirty thousand people who contacted him over a period of forty-three years.

A devout Christian, Edgar Cayce did not believe in reincarnation yet in his hypnotic state he would often indicate that the cause of a current ailment lay in the actions of an earlier lifetime and would then describe that period. He also forecast his own return in another body amidst the ruins of New York City. The records of his many thousands of 'readings' are maintained at the Association for Research and Enlightenment based in Virginia Beach in the United States.

At various stages in its evolution the human race has needed strong leadership, particularly after the demise of the Lemurian civilisation and the development of new races in Atlantis. At that point in time highly evolved beings from other planets and solar sysems volunteered to assist humanity. These advanced souls incarnated in physical forms, leading the people as their kings and emperors.

Our present civilisation also appears determined to self-destruct. In an effort to circumvent the unnecessary suffering and subsequent retardation of the race, highly evolved beings - known to mankind as the Ascended Masters of Love and Wisdom - are currently endeavouring to bring their influence to bear.

Those among us who are spiritually active and who can be encouraged to play a conscious role in stimulating the great shift of consciousness that the human race must undergo as it enters the Age of Aquarius, will begin to attract the attention of these

Illumined Ones. These are the same great souls who, in former times, inspired humanity.

The new Age of Aquarius will therefore be ushered in by those who are prepared to take the time to extend themselves, seeking to develop their latent spiritual qualities to the full. Every age has its share of oracles prophets and seers, for mankind is ever in need of spiritual guidance and direction.

Ascended Master, The Lady Mary

Although better known as the Mother of Jesus of Nazareth the World Teacher for the Age of Pisces, this Enlightened Being has also done much to aid mankind, and Her World Task for the New Age is already under way. She is the prime mover behind the emancipation of women but, in addition, those who desire to activate their seership abilities can obtain powerful assistance from this Ascended Master for She endeavours to encourage the development and expression of the feminine principle in our dual natures - that which listens to and carries out the Will of The Supreme Being.

CHAPTER THREE

SPIRITUAL AWAKENING

As we begin to awaken spiritually and to activate the qualities of the Soul, there is ever the query as to how we may know whether the communications received are of astral origin or not, or indeed, what part the conscious mind and the imagination may be playing in this activity. There are certain steps which the developing sensitive can take and provided that they do not at any time, consciously seek to become the channel for astral communications, then they should always receive truth.

All should however bear in mind the fact that the first test along the path of self-awareness lies in the necessity to practise discernment. Where the spiritual aspirant permits impatience to over-ride the nec essity for caution, and they then elect to take a seemingly swifter path toward enlightenment, then their endeavours may well come to grief, or they may at best become a psychic.

Always remember that it is never the hare that wins the spiritual race, but the tortoise (or the patient plodder) who slowly proceeds along The Way of Inner Enlightenment, carefully absorbing all that which they discover en-route and in this manner successfully attaining their spiritual goal.Before proceeding further, let me first illustrate the difference between the psychic and the true seer.

Psychics are those who are sensitive to forces not recognised by 'natural laws' and invariably are termed 'involuntary mediums'. In other words, they are not in control of their mediumistic abilities.

Their clairvoyant vision is often indistinct and many psychics can be rather vague when describing the colours or symbols they 'see' around another individual. As few among their number take the trouble to question their inspirers, or make any attempt to translate the imagery received, their 'visions' tend to add to the confusion of the person concerned.

Such sensitives easily establish contact with those souls who have recently departed the physical plane and in the process, all too often absorb the unpleasant vibrations many of their spirit communicators carry with them. Where the entity concerned departed the Earth Plane following a protracted period of suffering, or in a state of mental or emotional confusion, then the vibrations they still carry with them are rarely positive.

Although awareness of the measure of suffering which that entity may have undergone prior to physical death does serve to clearly identify the communicator, should the medium be unable to cast off those unpleasant vibrations, they may well suffer as the result.

Communications of this nature do of course serve to bring solace to the recently bereaved, but in my view they serve little purpose if, as the result, the channels themselves then become physically depleted or ill. Unfortunately, a great many psychics do do suffer for their cause, all too often undergoing a nervous breakdown, or suffering a cerebral haemmorhage, simply because they are forever 'on tap' and never know when to say 'no' to those who continually press them for some form of communication from a loved one.

Sensitives must always bear in mind that the earthly form is the robe of the soul and must be cared for in order to ensure a strong form in their next incarnation. What is more, those who demand such communications certainly will not die from the lack of one but the extremely sensitive medium may well die from one 'reading' too many.

The psychic must also bear in mind the Greater Law, and the possibility of encouraging the bereaved to become dependant, rather than encouraging such individuals to develop their own dormant abilities. If this occurs and those individuals then fail to pursue their personal destiny, then a Karma of Failure will eventuate with which the well intentioned psychic may become associated.

True Seers on the other hand will take the time and the trouble to develop their latent abilities slowly and in a constructive manner, learning to establish a link with those teachers who dwell on the higher sub-planes of the Mental Plane. To this end the most beneficial undertaking I can recommend is the practice of meditation at precisely the same time each day.

Thirty minutes will be sufficient, provided the exercise is approached in a disciplined manner, and always commences at precisely the same minute each and every day. In this way the aspirant may 'tune-in' to the 'rythmn of the universe' and those spirit entities whose task it is to train and instruct them will then utilise these occasions to communiicate. In this way the thirty minute period of meditation (or contemplation) becomes a potent growth experience.

Spiritual communications are received through the three upper chakras which correspond to the sixth and seventh senses. The chakras themselves are vortices or whirling wheels of light located within the first of our 'subtle bodies' , known as the Etheric Body or the Vital Body - a field of electromagnetic particles which immediately surrounds our physical form. (See page 108)

This non-physical form is composed of a kind of matter, the particles of which are finer than those from which our physical bodies are formed. The Etheric Body serves to protect the earthly form from attack by negative energies a task it achieves with the aid of the various colour rays we absorb from the ethers.

Each individual ray of colour provides the body with a form of energy - termed 'prana' in eastern philosophies, which serves to sustain both the etheric and the physical bodies. The chakras are the means by which these colourful energies are absor-

Chakra	Associated With

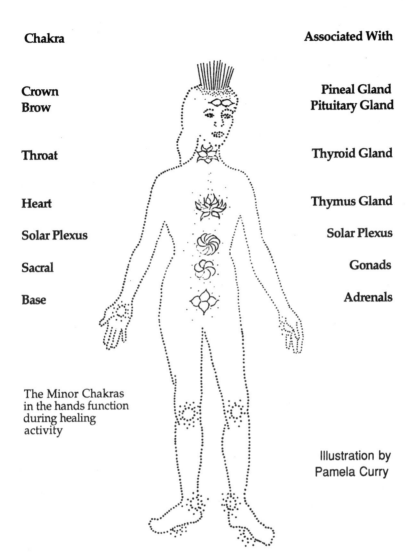

Crown — Pineal Gland
Brow — Pituitary Gland

Throat — Thyroid Gland

Heart — Thymus Gland

Solar Plexus — Solar Plexus

Sacral — Gonads

Base — Adrenals

The Minor Chakras
in the hands function
during healing
activity

Illustration by
Pamela Curry

**The Major and Minor Chakra Points
and the related Endocrine Glands**

bed each chakra responding to the vibration of a particular colour ray.

The Throat Chakra is situated in the Etheric Body parallel to the base of the throat in the physical form and is the seat of the sixth sense of Intuition (or the telepathic ability) whilst the seventh sense of Clairvoyance is reflected through the Brow and Crown Chakras.

Where individuals fail to activate the Crown Chakra, content to act upon that which they receive through the Brow or Throat Chakras, they tend to become psychics. These are individuals who are unable or unwilling to communicate with any plane of consciousness beyond the higher sub-plane of the Astral Realm.

When the Crown Chakra is stimulated into activity the awakening sensitive will begin to see flashing colours drawn from the higher end of the spectrum, but these will be observed only fleetingly and will be subject to constant change in hue giving the impression of gazing into a spiritual kaleidoscope.

Whilst some sensitives possess an objective clairvoyant ability, in that they can clearly perceive the non-physical dimensions whilst their physical eyes are open, the majority of clairvoyants tend to 'see' in a subjective manner. In other words they perceive clairvoyant images only when they close their eyes. However, the moment the sensitive begins to focus their conscious mind upon such phenomena, it invariably disappears.

Some individuals activate their spiritual talents quite easily, whilst others may experience a deal of difficulty in this direction. This is largely due to the current level of evolution of the individual concerned, for not all have attained that state of awareness where they may with ease, reactivate and utilise their spiritual senses. Indeed many individuals have deliberately blocked the expression of these abilities in former incarnations, or during the childhood of the current life experience due perhaps to an irrational fear of the unknown. Such behaviour does make the re-activation of the spiritual senses more difficult, but not impossible.

So how is communication with the non-physical realms effected? It is, of course, all a question of vibration. As solid matter is very heavy or dense its vibrational rate is extremely slow in comparison with that of the spirit self and the higher dimensions which are its true environment.

All is not as it may appear to our physical eyes and our planet, Earth, shares its point in space with the Astral Realm which, in common with all other planes, or levels of consciousness, has seven sub-planes each of which is as real and solid to those who inhabit them as this Plane of Matter is to you or me. The seventh or lowest sub-plane of the Astral Plane is what many Christians would term hell or purgatory, depending on their point of view and the experiences they assume await them there.

It is to this point that all must come following the death of the physical self, there to review the events of the life experience so recently completed. Following this the recently deceased must then compare its attainments (or failures) with the plan created in advance of incarnation by the Over-Self (which is the Reality) a record of which is maintained in the Hall of Records.

The soul will soon see that much was left incomplete and lessons will have to be repeated at some future point in time. There is no hall of judgment and for that matter no hell fire and eternal damnation as suggested by some belief systems.

Many souls who arrive at this point are confused. Aware that they have undergone the death experience yet puzzled to discover that they still live, albeit in a dimension which appears to be similar to the world they so recently departed.

During the process of transition the soul has not undergone any major transformation nor has it been accorded great wisdom. It is still the same individual with precisely the same level of awareness it possessed whilst in physical form.

Once they have adjusted to their new dimension they may begin the slow progress toward the higher sub-planes of the astral realm, depending upon the quality of recent life experiences and their success or failure therein.

However where its most recent physical experience has been a dismal failure, a life wherein self-interest has predominated, the soul must make retribution by spending a period of time upon an illusionary dimension, one fashioned from the negative thought patterns and emotional indulgences of that lifetime. This unpleasant environment will be populated by like minded souls and could be likened to hell or purgatory. Once the soul has accepted the error of their ways and sought to make amends they will be directed to their rightful Plane of Being, there to prepare for yet another incarnation.

Beyond the Astral Plane lies the Mental Plane which is the fifth Plane of Consciousness. This also has seven sub-planes. On the highest of these we may contact the Bearers of Light, teachers who endeavour to guide the steps of mankind. It is to this level of consciousness that developing mediums wisely direct their thoughts, requesting inspiration from this level and beyond, whilst refusing to accept any communication which has *originated* on the Astral Plane.

Many people question me on this point feeling that it is wrong to refuse communication. In reply I would ask: "What is it that you (as a sensitive) seek to achieve? Do you want to grow or merely to play as would a child ?" It is not at all difficult to communicate with the inhabitants of the Astral Plane, for it shares the same point in space with earth. As I have also indicated elsewhere, physical death does not mean the automatic granting of wisdom or enlightenment.

During its *initial* stage of 're- awakening' the soul has no greater knowledge than it had acquired prior to physical death, other than it now *knows* that death is but another illusion. As they lack the

greater knowledge we seek, why bother to communicate with those who have nothing of value to
convey?

There are some who do not share my opinion
who point to the fact that we have all experienced
many incarnations prior to the current lifetime.
They assume (erroneously) that knowledge of our
entire past is automatically restored following
physical death.   However the conscious mind -
which survives the death process - has no awareness of previous embodiments and subconscious
memory will not be reactivated until each individual soul acknowledges the errors of the most recent
incarnation and is prepared to make amends.

Beyond the Mental Plane lie the sixth and seventh
planes of consciousness and upon each successive
sub-plane thereof the vibration is purer, the light
more intense and the inhabitants infinitely more
evolved.

The Spiritual Hierarchy is located upon these higher planes but the spiritual aspirant who desires to
communicate with the Ilumined Ones, must first
earn the right to do so.   Discernment is the first test
encountered by the aspirant on the path of spiritual
attainment and failure to discern between illusion
and reality can have far reaching consequences.

According to the Ascended Master D. K. (known
also as The Tibetan Master) there are in existence
on the Astral Plane thought forms which manifest
in the image of the Ascended Masters. Such astral
forms are fashioned from the wishful thought
patterns of those who have read of the existence

of these Illumined Beings. These forms however are mere illusions and are not in any way connected with the Ascended Masters. The unwary may well be fooled by the commands such astral forms give.

The Ancient Wisdom however tells us that the Ascended Masters will never at any time issue commands to any of their disciples for to do so would be to rob them of their Divine gift of free will. The Illumined Ones will endeavour to inspire the aspirant, at times even indicating a possible course of action, but on every occaision the final decision will be made by the individual concerned.

Speaking from personal experience; on the few occaisions when I have been fortunate enough to receive inspiration from the Master Ragoczy, the undertakings He has asked me to contemplate have not always accorded with my desire (my Leonine ego intruding.) On each occasion however, it has always been left to me to mull the matter over, and finally to make my own decision.

Those who are slowly reactivating their spiritual potential could be likened to children undertaking their first term at school. There they are taught in the simplest of ways by those who are specifically trained to do so. They are not taught advanced mathematics by a university professor!

In a similar manner during our initial awakening period we will attract toward us those spirit teachers whose role it is to patiently encourage us in our spiritual unfoldment. With so much basic knowledge to re-acquire and dormant skills to re-activate there is little likelihood of receiving advanced instruction from highly evolved beings, for like attracts like.

Genuine seekers are constantly in search of truth. They are forever extending their horizons in a bid to communicate with the higher planes of consciousness from whose inhabitants they might gather greater knowledge. The seer should then endeavour to share their newly acquired truths with those drawn to them by the light in their aura.

If you want to become a true Seer, then each and every day determine to become a clearer channel than you were the previous day ensuring that the information you share with others, will be of such a nature that it will stimulate within them a need for greater growth.

Seers always endeavour to identify the latent qualities of the spirit possessed by each person drawn to them. The individuals concerned may have little or no knowledge of these qualities but once identified, that person should be encouraged to develop and express their spiritual talents. In this manner the Seer becomes a mirror providing a true reflection of each individual's personal destiny.

Where mediumistic abilities are abused in a bid to acquire power over others or used simply for material gain and where such actions then encourage the development of a dependancy upon that channel for constant guidance or direction the medium concerned will pay dearly for such actions at some future point in time. Be warned; the use of spiritual qualities brings great responsibility in its wake, far greater perhaps than might be imagined.

For those who seriously desire spiritual growth and are prepared to take the long, tortuous path toward enlightenment, I offer some practical sugestions which will certainly serve to enhance their level of awareness.

The Age of Aquarius (also referred to as The Age of the Mind and the Sciences) is exacting much of mankind particularly on the mental level. Its influence is already evident in the speed at which computer technology has been adopted world-wide particularly among the young. These new technologies owe much to the humble quartz crystal.

The use of crystals is not new for they were widely used during the Age of Gemini by the Atlantean civilisation. That knowledge has been jealously guarded by the priesthood of various cultures since that time but now, as the human race faces the task of shifting its level of consciousness (embracing thereby the Fourth Dimension) this knowledge is resurfacing once more.

In the light of this, I strongly recommend that all potential Seers utilise quartz crystals in their spiritual undertakings for such usage will certainly serve to speed up their spiritual momentum.

The energy output of single-pointed quartz crystals correspond with the vibrational level of the chakras but as every single crystal has its own specific energy output the spiritual aspirant must first discover which of their chakras responds to a particular crystal.

This is easily achieved. Simply hold the crystal in

the *left* hand, positioned slightly below the base of the Throat Chakra and project a continuous thought pattern of *'Love'* to its indwelling elemental intelligence. In turn this basic life form will respond to your loving input by intensifying the energy outflow from the crystal which will first be experienced as a cool tingling flow of energy or pressure in the region of the throat. This will then flow onwards into the chakra with which it is aligned.

Where for instance, the energy output of the crystal corresponds with the vibrational level of the Brow Chakra, the recipient will experience pressure or heat, even pain in the centre of the brow.

However, if its energy output corresponds with that of the Crown Chakra, the sensitive will then experience a deal of pressure atop the head.

If the energy exchange is noted only in the region of the throat then that crystal can be utilised in a bid to stimulate the intuitive faculty.

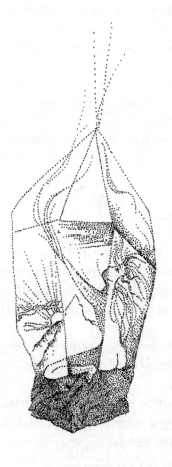

The Crystal Elemental

In accordance with *the* great spiritual law which states that *'in order to receive, you must first give of self '* those who desire true inspiration must be prepared to play a part in the continuing evolution of the planet. (Undertaken prior to daily meditation this is a relatively simple exercise "comprising" a short period spent in the healing of the earth).

This is not at all difficult to achieve, for we are all creators in our own right and whatever we think takes form in the ethers with the aid of The Lords of Form. . . (Ethereal beings whose task it is to fashion form from the energy mankind releases as thought into the ethers)

Sit comfortably and endeavour to imagine that you are far out in space. Visualise if you can the Earth far beneath you and direct toward it a ray of pure *White Light* . Focus this upon and around the planet. . . Maintain this projection of 'light' until you are able to 'sense' or 'see' the outer etheric counterpart of the planet suffused with radiant light.

The period spent utilising the power of thought in this constructive manner will aid both the planet and the self, for that which is sent out on the ethers in this manner will eventually return to its creator who will in turn receive a measure of enlightenment.

Follow this by visualising a great flame of Violet Light high above the earth and direct this toward all areas of conflict upon the planet. Focus this cleansing flame upon the warlords who create or maintain conflict for their own ends regardless of the needs of the people. Having shared the Violet Flame in this manner, draw it into your home, filling the room in which you are sitting. You will gradually become aware of the potency of this powerful cleansing force as it begins to permeate the molecular structure of your physical body.

Consciously direct part of the flame into the Crown Chakra high atop the head. As this is the seat of the Spiritual Intelligence utilise its energy to activate this major centre for once this is fully activated you may, with great self discipline, attune to the teachers of the higher sub-plane of the Mental Plane and beyond.

Now focus the Violet Flame upon the Brow Chakra in the centre of the forehead, which in itself is the seat of the mind, but also the location of the lens of the inner eye. Once the Brow and Crown Chakras are open and fully operational you may then begin to 'see' with the eye of the soul

Now channel the flame into the Throat Chakra at the base of the throat. This is the seat of telepathic ability. The energy flow through this chakra is often blocked due to imbalance within its associated endocrine gland, the Thyroid. This imbalance is invariably due to persistent negative thinking so utilise the energy of the Violet Flame to purify both centres. To restore harmony here first focus the flame upon the Throat Chakra before directing it into the Thyroid Gland.

Proceed downward directing the flame now into the Heart Chakra which is the seat of the Soul and a centre that is rarely active. The vast majority of individuals incarnate today are still functioning via the egoic centre of the Solar Plexus and their loving relationships tend to be of a possessive nature.

The Heart Chakra is located in the centre of the breast and once this centre is open you will begin to express love for others in a totally unconditional manner. This in turn will eventually lead you toward a true understanding of what is meant by Christ Consciousness.

Transfer the Violet Flame to the Solar Plexus the seat of the Ego or Lower Will - a problem centre for most individuals particularly those who seek to expand their spiritual horizons. Use the Violet Flame in a bid to eradicate the long term effects of emotional imbalance and the abuse of the will from this most sensitive of centres. A tremendous sense of release will be experienced once the Refiner's Fire enters this centre.

Now move the flame downward into the Sacral Chakra located in the region of the navel. Pride and ambition find expression at this point which is also the seat of the lower (sexual) nature. This centre may therefore require a deal of attention.

Finally, focus that Violet Flame on the Base Chakra located at the base of the spine. Imbalance in this centre is often due to a sense of insecurity or to a lack of earthing, (particulary evident in those who are born on the 11th or 29th of a month and who tend to dream a great deal).

The Base Chakra is also associated with the bony framework of the physical form and a measure of imbalance here could also serve to forewarn of future health problems on that level.   (My earlier work Know Yourself - Heal Yourself deals more fully with the chakras.)

Having cleansed and stimulated every chakra with the Violet Flame, direct the flame back up the Etheric Spine towards the crown of the head, encouraging it to enter the Crown Chakra once more and then visualise this energy flowing downward from centre to centre further stimulating each of the chakras en route.

Once it reaches the Base Chakra visualise the flame then spreading out beyond your physical body into the Etheric Body cleansing it of any state of disharmony.

Then allow the flame to flow outward into the Emotional Body,purifying this of any destructive effects of uncontrolled emotions and finally, visualise that flame flowing

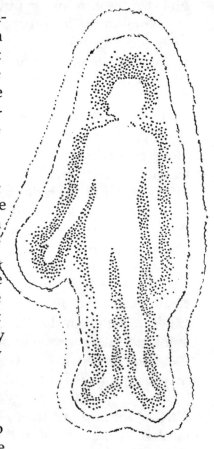

The Subtle Bodies

on into the Mental Body, cleansing this of the results of negative thinking.

To complete this exercise visualise the whole self, physical and non-physical, encapsulated in a flame of violet light, its powerful energies cleansing and stimulating every cell and atom within your being.

This visualisation exercise enables the spiritual aspirant to become one with the Violet Flame, and in turn, one with the Essence of The Ascended Master Ragoczy , who is The Lord of The Violet Flame. His current world task incorporates the stimulating of the sixth and seventh senses within those who are spiritually awakened, and then to encourage the use of these for the benefit of the human race. Those who follow this proceedure are certain to attract His attention.

Where spiritual aspirants sincerely desire to receive intuitive or clairvoyant communications from the highest sub-plane of the Mental Plane and beyond, then I really do suggest that they follow this exercise with the following affirmation, saying it aloud or thinking it clearly, so giving each word its full emphasis.

I Am
I Am all that I Am.
One with the Universal Mind,
One with the Source of All Life.
I Am one with all life forms,
And they are one with me.

J am love, J am light
J am Peace, J am "
Jn that which J am J invoke the light of the
Teachers of The higher sub plane, of the mental
Plane + beyond the refuse all communications
which origanate upon The Astral Plane
J AM

I Am Love,
I Am Light,
I Am Peace.
I Am.

In that which I Am I invoke the light of
the Teachers of the higher sub-plane of the
Mental Plane and beyond and refuse
all comunications which originate
upon the Astral Plane,
I Am

Where these preliminary exercises are carried out daily spiritual aspirants clearly signal their willingness to discipline the self. Then the spirit teachers endeavouring to guide their steps along the path of enlightenment will draw close, ensuring that the spiritual momentum of their charge continues apace. This in turn will result in the receiving of communications from the higher sub-plane of the the Mental Plane and beyond.

CHAPTER FOUR

THE MEANING
OF SYMBOLS

The initial activation of the Crown Chakra is often
heralded by a constantly changing flow of colour
which manifests the moment the individual sits
quietly or seeks to meditate. Eventually small symbolic images will begin to appear in the midst of
this restless flow of colour and the sensitive now
needs to be alert, and to carefully note every aspect
of the communication, that colourful radiance having a large part to play in this.

Where for instance you notice a **Large Eye** gazing at
you at you from within a ball of golden light it is an
indication that your actions are being observed and
that you will in due course receive enlightenment.
The eye of course represents the **All-Seeing-Eye** and
signifies the possession of a clairvoyant ability and
that this capacity is about to be stimulated anew.

All sensitives need to learn to translate that which
they 'see' clairvoyantly and also to enquire as to
whether or not their translation of a particular
image is correct. Where the symbol then reappears
the answer is that your translation is incorrect and
that the symbol requires further consideration.

In meditation or prayer we often ask for enlightenment so that we might deal with certain difficulties currently being experienced. In response we may then receive the symbol of **a Cross** surrounded by a deep **blue radiance.**

At first this may not appear to be the information requested - yet within it lies the required inspiration. Take careful note of the construction of that cross. Is this a wooden or metal cross, or has it been fashioned from light? All have quite different meanings.

Many people mistakenly look upon the symbol of the cross as an indication that a burden or a trial lies ahead unaware that it represents a tremendous esoteric challenge, for the cross signifies potential growth - provided the individual is prepared to undertake a measure of selfless service.

Where the cross appears to be of **roughly hewn wood** then the answer to the question is really quite easy. The way ahead lies in the undertaking of a humble service on behalf of humanity, utilising the intuitive faculty (identified by the blue radiance), in order to achieve this.

Should the cross be fashioned from **gold or silver** the individual is being advised to fulfill some form of 'spiritual service' to mankind, one wherein they can utilise their intuitive ability to guide others. The dormant sixth sense will, once it is fully activated, clearly indicate the form of assistance each person requires.

However, should that cross appear to consist of

radiant light then the nature of the service to be undertaken is one of enlightenment, the individual concerned taking the measure of truth they have discovered to date, and sharing this lovingly with others. This particular symbol indicates that the role of the teacher lies ahead, which may prove to be quite daunting during its initial stages.

An Abyss. To be lead to the edge of an abyss is a clear warning that those concerned have reached a point in life where a major decision must now be made. They can no longer continue along their present pathway and must decide whether to strive to forge an entirely new career, or possibly develop a different outlook upon life. The way ahead will be difficult and in order to succeed great determination and staying power will be required.

An Airliner can have ᵭ several meanings. It may represent an idealist, someone who needs to come down to earth or who is possessed of high flying ideals. It can equally serve to indicate the need to raise our level of consciousness beyond the norm - to determinedly soar toward the spiritual heights and to take many others - who may be less courageous with us.

Alpha and Omega. Symbolises the beginning and the end of a situation or an undertaking, the completion of a specific task and the commencement of something new. It is

always a very positive
directive for the spirit-
ual aspirant.

An Altar. Where this
symbol is received it is
a clear indication that
we must be prepared
to dedicate ourselves
to a Greater Will and
purpose. Once this
undertaking has been
accepted there can be
no turning back.

An Anchor can have
several meanings. If
life has been rather try-
ing and where it is evi-
dent that the anchor is
being raised it indi-
cates it is time to
weigh anchor and sail
away, leaving cares
behind.

However, where there has been a singular lack of
stability this symbol illustrates the need to drop anchor and seek some form of secure or safe haven.
Finally, it can also reflect the need to become an
anchor for someone who lacks direction and who
may be in need of a measure of strong support.

Animals are often depicted symbolically and are usually the simplest of symbols to translate. Always

look for the most practical translation of any symbol rather than for major esoteric interpretations.

A Bull charging (toward you) relates to determined opposition in a particular field of endeavour. This comes as a warning to take swift, evasive action.

A Cockerel crowing clearly identifies the role of the person concerned. This is to become a Herald of the New Age crowing aloud the knowledge they have acquired in a bid to draw the attention of humanity to the dawning of the Age of Change.

The Crab - with pincers extended represents a possessive individual who may have designs on you or your worldly wealth.

The Donkey is extremely simple to translate, for it indicates a measure of stubbornness in the querant, a weakness requiring immediate attention.

The Ankh, in ancient Egypt was considered to be a key; the key to Greater Wisdom. A symbolic representation of total self mastery and the controlled

use of power. The ankh was awarded only to the Master Initiates who, through great self discipline and humility, acknowledged the part they were to play in the greater Cosmic Plan. It is a symbol which represents eternal or enduring life and is not one to trifle with.

Should the symbol of the **Ankh** or **Looped Cross** be seen on the side of a pyramid it represents the attainment of a former incarnation wherein the individual strove to become the Master Initiate. This symbol serves to indicate the need for greater self discipline if that goal is to be attained in the present lifetime.

The Anvil clearly indicates that something requires hammering out, and that the querant should be prepared to be receptive in a given situation even though it may be far from pleasant.

An Apple represents a desire for knowledge, usually of the occult kind, or the need to go in search of truth. Many difficulties or obstacles lie ahead on the the way to its attainment

A Basket, often filled with flowers or fruit, comes as an expression of love from those on the non-physical dimensions. Flowers indicate appreciation for past endeavours on behalf of others, whilst fruit signifies that the recipient may soon taste the fruits of their labours.

A Bell is a signal from the Higher Self that it is time to commence 'sounding our 'note' in the ethers. This occurs when we reactivate latent spiritual tal-

ents and begin to share
these with mankind.
Our spiritual momen-
tum then increases
resulting in a partic-
ular sound or 'note'
which can be heard on
all Planes of Consci-
ousness, attracting to-
ward us those who
may be of assistance.

Birds - of all sizes and varieties are often given as a
symbolic indication of situations that lie ahead

The Dove represents
someone who has in-
carnated in a bid to
become a Bearer of
Peace and Light. It also
identifies Jehova or
The Divine Spirit and
is an indication that a
spiritual gift or quality
is about to be reactiv-
ated.

The Eagle is always a
forewarning of a major
initiation, or cleansing
experience ahead. A
golden eagle sitting on
a rock, closely observ-
ing us, is an early
warning that difficult-
ies lie ahead, whilst an

eagle hovering overhead indicates that these are imminent.

Where the image is that of a **White Eagle,** it represents that great evolved being who utilises this image as a form of identification. This is the overseer for all who share their healing skills with humanity, whether within the established medical field, fringe medicines, or in natural healing. This symbol is an indication that the individual is currently under observation and soon will undergo a major test of faith. Further progress in this field will be blocked until this situation has been dealt with.

The Owl was considered by the ancient Chinese to be a very wise bird because it could see in the dark, and a vision of an owl can indicate the presence of a spirit helper of Chinese origin. In the vast majority of cases it serves to indicate the possession of a dormant clairvoyant capacity which we should now endeavour to develop.

The Peacock comes as a grim warning for those who have permitted the ego to take over and who boast of their spiritual attainments. This warning should not be ignored for it indicates that the pit of spiritual pride lies ahead. It symbolises potential failure with regard to the second of the Major Initiations.

The Raven is linked to seership but is a symbol with a deeply occult meaning. It serves to represent the commencement of a seven year period of initiation wherein the querant must be prepared to become the Messenger of the Gods, identified by the raven. This is the first of the seven major initiations and indicates a person with great spiritual potential.

The Swan is ever a symbol indicating the need for inner peace. The White Swan gliding on the still waters of a lake indicates the ability to reach down into the subconscious (the lake) and to bring to light long forgotten aspects of truth.

The White Swan also symbolises the Fourth Initiation which awaits those who go in'search of' the mythical Grail. This is the quest for Greater-Self awareness and may only be attained when the aspirant is in control of their powers of sympathy and antipathy, permitting no unconscious predjudice to influence their everyday actions.

The Fourth Initiation entails the 'giving up' of all

material possessions with the aspirant being prepared to travel to various parts of the world as
and when directed by their spirit helpers, there to
share the light of truth with their fellow men and
women.

Conversely, **The Black Swan** comes as a warning,
serving to identify a servant of the black arts. No
matter how calm or gentle their exterior may be,
they are allied to the darker forces and all aspirants
should heed the warning being conveyed by this
symbol and avoid such individuals.

To be shown many **Books** is a request from the Over
Self to begin to study what is hidden in a bid to extend our spiritual horizon.

A Bow and Arrow rel-
ates to personal aspira-
tion and the necessity
for great determination
if we are to succeed
in attaining a desired
goal in life. This sym-
illustrates the necess-
ity for patience, avoid-
ance of hasty decisions,
and the need for great
care when aiming for
a target.

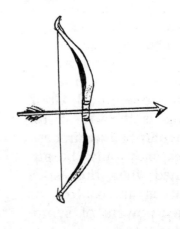

A Box represents something that is hidden from or
unknown to the person concerned. It can be translated in several ways, for it can relate to a situation
that lies ahead, or to an aspect of the self. Either

way it indicates that something must be opened up or revealed to public gaze.This symbol may also represent a warning with regard to becoming 'boxed in' within a particular situation or undertaking. However should that box be tied with ribbons it relates to a pleasant surprise ahead. An open and discarded box on the otrher hand can indicate that something valued or hidden from others has been discovered.

A Bull - see under animals.

Bridges may be shown when life is filled with difficulties or there is a need for change either materially or spiritually. At such times a bridge represents an opportunity to surmount current obstacles.

The Butterfly represents those who possess a bright and lighthearted approach toward life but who nonetheless may prove to be rather shallow; someone who refuses to accept any measure of responsibility, moving swiftly onward to taste fresh delights once a relationship or undertaking becomes too

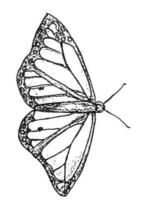

onerous. The ancients on the other hand, considered that the butterfly represented the soul and its desire to seek the light.

The Caduceus or winged staff around which two serpents are entwined represents some one with healing potential, an individual who, at some point in their past has utilised healing powers. This symbol is an indication of their destiny; to dedicate the self to healing of mind and body.

The Candle is a very simple representation of light and reflects the early stages of spiritual development in the aspirant. Where the candle is unlit the individual should be encouraged to ignite the flame of spiritual aspiration once more, overcoming any aspect of self doubt in order to take this simple light (or truth) to mankind. If the candle is already lit and burning brightly it indicates someone who is already committed to a simple service of enlightenment to mankind.

A Candle reflecting its **Light Upon a Cross.** The candle represents the light of compassion which the person concerned must endeavour to cast upon the difficulties experienced by others. These individuals accomplish their tasks, often unnoticed and unsung on the highways and byways of life

A Candelabra is an ancient symbol for enlightenment, and the number of branches it has indicates the form this service should take. Two branches correspond to the need for total adaptability when endeavouring to assist others, and to use the feminine aspect of the self; ie: intuition and clairvoyance, to do so.

Four branches would indicate the necessity for an ex tremely down-to-earth and practical approach when endeavouring to enlighten others, whilst the seven branched candelabra represents the casting of light upon occult or metaphysical subjects. *(See chapter 6 dealing with numeric factors)*

A Cannon. This symbol comes as a warning that opposition lies ahead and that certain individuals are preparing to bring forward the big guns determined to block further advancement. Here the advice is to hold fast to your beliefs; accept the necessity for the opposition which lies before you and ask ' on high' for inspiration on how to deal with the situation.

A Cave high in a rock face indicates the measure of difficulty which lies ahead of those who desire to expand their level of consciousness. The cave and what lies hidden within it may appear to be beyond reach but with great determination , this can be attained.

The Centaur. This symbol (half man, half horse) comes as a warning that the lower nature is obstructing the attainment of Higher-Self goals. Time to bring the lower senses under the firm control of the Soul

A Chalice or **Jewelled Cup** provides an indication of the evolution of the soul to date.Take careful note of the appearance of the cup, the jewels thereon representing the qualities of the spirit which are to be utilised in the task ahead.

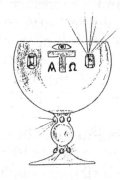

This symbol should not be treated lightly, for it reflects the potential to become the 'Cup Bearer of the Light' once more. This is an extremely onerous task, one which the individual has fashioned from past attainment, times when they went in search of truth and then courageously shared this with others.

A Champagne Glass, full and raised in salute is an obvious and positive symbol indicating that a joyous celebration lies ahead.

The Chariot and Charioteer represent the triumph of the higher self (the charioteer) over the lower self (the horse-drawn chariot). It indicates a long battle successfully overcome.

Chickens - recently hatched, represent a fresh undertaking or a new way of life. The number of chicks shown is always important. For instance, one chick represents an independent role ahead whilst two chicks indicate the need to utilise the feminine aspect in that role. (See chapter 6 - Numeric Factors)

Quite often the symbol of a **Child** or a **Babe in Arms**, tended by a spirit helper is given and represents a long held desire about to bear fruit, or an opportunity for growth that lies ahead. When the time is right, this 'child' of your ambition will be presented to you, but until then it is being nurtured on the higher planes of consciousness. This comes as a forewarning of personal responsibility ahead.

The Cloister: To be lead into a cloister is an indication that ahead lies a situation which will demand total spiritual commitment ie: the individual will be expected to dedicate the remainder of their life to the public expression of their beliefs.

The Clown can have several meanings. It can indicate the presence of a spirit helper who comes in this guise in a bid to dispel despair at times of difficulty, or it can represent the need to raise the spirits of others, when all is dark around and about them.

A Cockerel - see under animals.

A Column of Stone is an indication of the spiritual stature of the person concerned identifying them as those who, by the strength of their belief and actions, support others. An example of what is meant here is when Jesus of Nazareth spoke of the future of the Apostles saying that "they would become pillars within the temple and would go out no more. . ." Two columns and the space between them are said to be a representation of the way toward eternity.

The Cornucopia or the Horn of Plenty is a clear indication that the person for whom this is seen is soon to reap the benefits of their past endeavours.

A Crab - see under animals.

A Crashing Plane is a dire warning,for it represents high flying ideals or impractical ideas which are about to come to grief.

The Crocodile is a timely warning that destructive forces lie in wait ahead,partly submerged in the shallow waters of psychic undertakings.

A Crossroads with a signpost at its centre has

more than one mean-
ing. There is the ob-
vious translation indi-
cating the necessity to
reach a decision as to
which path you will
now follow. Or it can
represent a role which
lies ahead, ie to become
the one who shows the
way by providing ad-
vice or guidance to
those who have reach-
ed a point of decision
in their life.

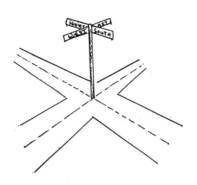

A Crow comes as a warning that someone who utilises dark forces is seeking to tap into your thoughts.
In the former Atlantean civilisation the black magicians used large black birds to fly out and observe
certain individuals, later communicating their
findings telepathically to their evil masters. This is
a symbol which forewarns of the necessity to be
ever vigilant and to keep one's own counsel, trust-
ing no-one, and should a crow be observed upon
the path ahead, it is a timely warning that a dark
force lies in wait.

A Crown is invariably
a symbolic representat-
tion of great responsib-
ility ahead. If heavily
jewelled it represents
the necessity to utilise
the qualities of the spi-
rit (represented by the

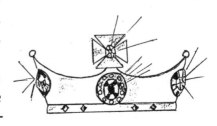

gems that adorn it) to fulfill that undertaking.

A Silver Cup, covered
by a cloth, from under
which a great light radi-
ates. 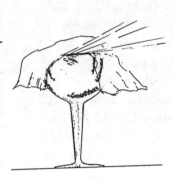 This is the age-old
representation of the
Grail Cup, indicating
the eternal search for
Self, upon which the
individual must now
be prepared to embark
(once more!)

A **Daffodil** is the Herald of Spring, a period
when nature casts
aside the dark days of
winter.  At such a time
the daffodil provides
great upliftment and
this symbol illustrates
the role ahead of the
person for whom it is
given.This is to go out and trumpet aloud the truth,
advising others that the dark days are drawing to an
end and a new Golden Age is about to dawn.

A Deer watching from a distance, represents the
sixth sense or intuitive capacity which may with
great determination, be activated once more. However, if the deer is fleeing it reveals that there is a
deal of fear with regard to the use of this talent.

A Desert can have several meanings. It can represent what lies ahead. A barren period that must be prepared for. It can also indicate that it is time for the individual to go out into the wilderness "and there seek for the truth which lies deep within the self". Like the prophets of the past, they must turn aside from all material pleasures and prepare to do battle with the self.

Desolate Scene. This invariably corresponds with an unpleasant phase of life that lies ahead. Such situations always reflect a period of test or initiation and the person concerned should be advised to accept (the situation and the necessity for it,) and then ask The Creator for inspiration on how to deal with it.

A **Dog** symbolises a protective and faithful friend (who may or may not be in a physical form). This comes to reassure the individual that despite what they may assume, they are not alone.

A **Donkey** - see under animals

A **Door** standing open represents an opportunity which is there for the taking. A **closed door** on the other hand indicates that the individual cannot proceed along their desired pathway, whilst **a door which is partially ajar** suggests that a situation previously blocked, is now open to those who have the courage to push onwards. **Two doors** on the path ahead indicate that there is a need to make a choice in a future action.

To be taken to the **Door** of a **Church or Temple** indicates that the individual has reached a point in life where they must be prepared to commit to a belief or an ideal.

The Dragon represents a warning particularly where it is belching fire and smoke. It represents the destructive thought forces this individual is unleashing into the ethers to the detriment of self and others and they should be counselled about the long-term effects of such thought patterns.

However, if the dragon is quite passive it symbolises the Ley energy or Dragon Power, indicating a former life as a geomancer and here the symbol suggests that this person should consider studying earth energies once more with the aim of working with the Ley power and the Elemental Kingdom for the benefit of the planet and mankind. (Ley energy is a force that flows through the earth at times of solstice and equinox and which was utilised by the ancients in in their fertility rites.)

Eagles - see under Birds.

Eastern Temple. This symbol may be given in a bid to reawaken memory of a former lifetime spent in meditative silence in such a temple, a life experience which may have a part to play in the present incarnation. It may also serve to indicate the presence of a spirit helper of eastern origin.

An Eye : See page 39

An Egg can represent a fresh opportunity, its true nature hidden from view (the shell) but before this new way of life (the chick) manifests, a great deal of patience will be required.

The Elephant is an indi cation of a difficult task ahead, one which may require great strength. This symbol can also indicate the presence of a spirit helper of Indian origin (where the elephant has no tusks) who comes to assist with the difficulties which lie ahead.

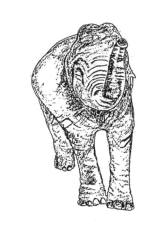

The Field represents the mind and a field that is filled with weeds indicates a mind which must be be brought under the firm control of the Higher Self.

A Freshly Ploughed Field on the other hand represents a mind from which the weeds of ignorance have been eliminated and prepared for the

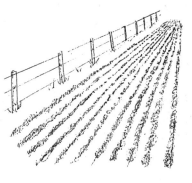

sowing of seeds of truth.

A Field of Corn filled with red poppies reveals a growing harvest of spiritual truth (the corn) amidst which many deeply materialistic or emotional thought patterns still find expression (the poppies). It will be necessary for this person to endeavour to overcome any thoughts which relate to lower-self desires if they are to make any worthwhile spiritual progress.

A Blazing Fire can ind-icate a volatile person-ality, someone who blows hot and cold in their friendships. Above all, this is a specific warning of the necessity to control a fiery temperament.

To be offered a **Flag or Standard** indicates that the individual must now be prepared to publicly declare a deeply held belief and to defend it at all costs. Quite often the standard is shown as a white silken banner trimmed with gold braid upon which a large eye appears. This represents the Standard of the Father/Mother God which dark forces may well attempt to tear down or destroy.

Flowers also feature prominently in symbolic com-munications for they mean so much to mankind. Here are some which are frequently given symbol-ically.

Pansies always represent thoughts directed
toward those on the
earth-plane, by those
who now dwell upon
another dimension.
This symbol usually
comes as a form of
rememberance, or to
thank someone for
deeds undertaken in
the past.

Forget-Me-Nots are easily translated, coming from
one who is still bound by ties of love to those upon
the earth plane.

However, if shown an
Orchid it comes as a
clear warning to avoid
the person with whom
they are associated ind-
icating someone who
serves the dark forces.
This should *not* be
taken to infer that
those who cultivate
orchids are involved
in dark practices.

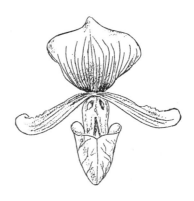

A White Arum Lily is a symbol with powerful
Egyptian overtones, for in ancient Egypt this served
to represent the female initiate who was wedded to
the white arts and the path of light. We have all
followed the magical path at some point in the past,

a pathway on which only the strong succeed.

When shown this symbol for another person, it is an indication that the feminine aspect of their dual nature, (which listens to the Will of The Creator) is active and that they have recently passed a major initiation in their pursuit of truth.

To be taken into **a Forest** is an indication that the spiritual path is blocked ahead by all manner of difficulties and obstacles, and that at times there will be no clear pathway in sight. This comes as a warning to be ever vigilant, lest the path toward truth or reality is overlooked at a time of much inner conflict.

The Fountain is another symbol representing the feminine principal of our dual nature (the sensitive, intuitive aspect). This symbol indicates the necessity to develop the quality of mercy and of the need to listen more attentively to the still inner voice. On the higher planes of consciousness this symbol also represents the female initiate.

A Fox is a symbolic representation of a wily and cunning adversary who may be stalking you, or those dependant upon you. A time to be vigilant and to prepare for the unexpected.

An Open Gate beyond which lies a field or fields, indicates that an obstacle to progress is being removed, and that a fresh field of activity is opening before you. It symbolises a new beginning.

A bunch of Grapes has deep occult meaning. The grapes represent the fruit of the Divine Twins Arbal Jesus and Arbel Jesus. Green grapes represent the feminine aspect and black grapes, the masculine. The colour of the grapes indicates which aspect of this Divine Being you were associated with in the past. Arbel Jesus (the feminine aspect) appeared as The Nazarene, whilst Arbal Jesus is said to have incarnated as John The Baptist.

To be shown **a Hand,** palm extended toward you, is an offer of help or assistance from those upon the non-physical dimensions who are concerned about a situation currently being experienced. If there is an eye in the centre of the palm the indication is that clairvoyant direction will be given.

The image of a **Harp** has special significance indicating an ability to become a rather unique instrument (or channel) for spiritual communications. It also signifies the necessity for great self discipline in order to attune to the higher planes of consciousness. This symbol also has strong links with The Ascended Master Ragoczy in his former incarnation as Merlin the Enchanter.

The Hawk is an ancient representation of The Christ Force and is linked with Horus, the Son of Isis and Osiris who led the first divine dyn-

asty of ancient Egypt. Horus represented the Christ Light and this symbol is often an indication of association with the Temple of Horus in the past.

The Herald with banner flying trumpeting aloud, indicates the role ahead for the person concerned, to come into the forefront of life and awaken others to the need for change in their outlook or lifestyle. The New Age is upon us and many are still unaware of the dramatic changes this will bring.

Herbs. To be shown herbs growing in a garden or together with a mortar and pestle, are an indication that one should study the use of herbs, particularly with regard to their healing properties.

A Hermit indicates the necessity for a deal of study, and a measure of isolation from the world in a bid to master self and to perfect your spiritual skills.

Horses relate to the thought patterns of mankind. Always take careful note of colouring and activity for this has a major part to play in the correct translation of this symbol.

A **White Horse** waiting patiently, represents thoughts of a spiritual nature which are firmly under control, whilst a **Brown Horse** is an indication of 'earthy' thought patterns or a tendency to indulge in thoughts of an earthy

nature.

A Grey Horse represents fearful thought patterns, which should be brought under firm control if you wish to avoid an unpleasant situation ahead, or subsequent illhealth, whilst **A Black Horse** indicates thoughts which are dark or unpleasant; perhaps destructive.

If the horse is wild or unruly, in need of taming, then thought patterns are out of control and need to be reined in to avoid confusion in life. The colour of the horse will illustrate the nature of the thought patterns which are in need of control.

Where there is **a Rider upon the Horse** it indicates that the Higher Self is now in control and disciplining the everyday thought process. It can also signify that the Spirit Mentor seeks to encourage a measure of discipline with regard to thought.

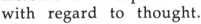

A Horse attached to a Plough, slowly ploughing a field indicates that thought patterns are firmly under control and that the mind (the field) is being prepared for the seeds of truth and a subsequent spiritual harvest.

A series of **Hurdles** upon the spiritual path represents a number of obstacles which you will have to clear in order to attain your objective.

An image of **An Island** on the far horizon is often an answer to a plea to be shown the way ahead, and serves to identify a personal goal. You need to set sail for deeper waters, in search of the spiritual truths that lie hidden deep beneath the surface.

The Key is an ancient symbol, one which is relatively easy to translate. It indicates that the person for whom this is shown is about to be given the key to a problem which blocks the path ahead. Note the nature of the key, whether it is of iron, silver or gold, for this serves to illustrate the nature of the obstacle ahead.

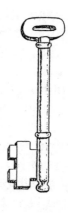

An Iron Key provides the answer to one of the many difficulties we must all experience in everyday life. Where the key is surrounded in a glowing green radiance it indicates that, with an harmonious outlook, all current difficulties can be resolved.

Silver or **Golden Keys** relate to the unlocking of the door of spiritual endeavour, serving to indicate that the door to the ancient mysteries or higher awareness lies before you.

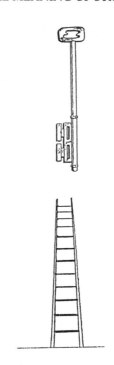

A Ladder is frequently given symbolically, either as a rope ladder or a wooden ladder of blue hue. It indicates that an opportunity to raise your level of consciousness is being offered.

A **Rope Ladder** illustrates that a somewhat precarious ascent can be anticipated in the search for higher awareness, whilst **a Blue Ladder** serves to illustrate just how this can be achieved ie: by constructive use of the intuitive ability, step by step toward greater awareness.

A **Lake** represents the unknown or the spiritual depths, and to be shown a lake indicates the need for attainment of inner tranquility which can best be achieved by the daily practice of meditation.

A **Still Lake** surrounded by **snow capped mountains** indicates a need to withdraw from the hurly-burly of life in a bid to become still and to develop a measure of serenity, for a major challenge lies ahead(the snow capped mountains) which in themselves represent the need to extend your current level of consciousness, and be prepared for all manner of hardship enroute.

A Lamb is an ancient symbol, one which has several meanings. It can indicate the necessity for purity of thought and simplicity of purpose or the need to be meek in the face of determined opposition.

The general translation of this symbol is for the individual to be prepared to become the sacrificial lamb in a particular scenario or undertaking, which then may lead to a new way of life. Alternatively, this symbol could be representative of this person's outlook on life, feeling that they are ever the sacrificial lamb.

A Lamp is often a directive of the need to learn to protect the flame of truth to ensure that it cannot be extinguished at the first puff of the

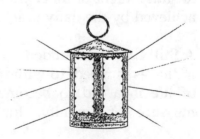

wind of opposition and to then take this light out and share it with mankind.

The symbol of **Light** (in various forms) is often given in answer to a plea to be shown the way ahead. A blazing **Ball of Light** is an indication that our plea has been heard and that enlightenment will be given. Similarly, a **Ray of Light** is a response to prayers and is a confirmation that you are neither alone or forgotten.

The Lighthouse repre-sents the individual who must be prepared to be strong in the face of adversity, who remains steadfast in the face of the storms which will rage about. They must determined-ly beam out the light of truth, forewarning others of the dangers that lie ahead.

At times the symbol of **A Lion** is given and this can represent over-whelming strength of character, personality, or the will. It is the task of the sensitive to trans-late this symbol corr-ectly.

As a dominating will or personality can lead to conflict in the immediate environment, the person concerned must be forewarned of this, particularly when shown the symbol of a **Rampant Lion,** for this serves to indicate a personality which is destroying its environment.

To be shown **Loaves of Bread** is a clear indication of the need to go out and feed the multitude with those truths you have found to be so meaningful.

A Lotus Blossom represents the awakening of the spiritual nature, with the Crown Chakra becoming active. It symbolises the Higher Self re-awakening. As knowledge begins to permeate the mind, illuminating the path to the God-Head, the blossom will slowly unfold.

A Lyre (in common with the harp and the violin) denotes a potential for trance mediumship . As the seven strings of the lyre are said to represent the seven sacred planets, this symbol could also indicate an ability to channel the music of the higher spheres. For a musician it may represent a bid to encourage expansion of consciousness and attunement with the Music Temples in those higher dimensions.

To be shown **A Mask** may indicate the necessity to mask your feelings or hide one's true intentions in a particular undertaking. It can also relate to another person who has not revealed their true identity or nature.

To be shown **A Mirror** indicates that you should take a long, clear look at self and at your intentions, gaining valuable insights thereby. It can also mean that you should endeavour to see your actions from anothers point of view.

A Monkey can either relate to an individual with a mischievous nature, or to another person who may well prove to be destructive. This is a symbol which indicates the need for caution when dealing with certain people.

The Moon can reflect the necessity to discipline wayward emotions. As the moon also relates to our feminine aspect it can also indicate the need

to develop a dormant mediumistic ability.

Mountains are always a clear signal of the need to prepare for the task of raising our level of consciousness beyond the norm. Although some may see this as a welcome challenge it may not be as simple as it may appear. Be prepared for obstacles along the way.

A Pathway Through Mountains indicates that a clearly defined pathway, leading toward higher states of consciousness lies ahead enabling you to more readily overcome the obstacles this journey presents.

A Snow Covered Mountain Peak serves to identify a major challenge that lies immediately ahead, representing your personal peak of endeavour.

A range of **Snow Covered Mountains** suggests

that obstacles lie ahead of those seeking to raise their level of consciousness. The snow and ice indicating just how difficult the final stage of this task will be.

Thick Mud or Slime upon the pathway ahead, is a clear warning to proceed with a great deal of caution and to avoid becoming enmeshed in emotional situations. A narrow track around a muddy area suggests that this situation may be sidestepped.

A Needle and Cotton drawing together worn threads, identifies a major challenge ahead. It symbolises the need to repair the threads of a damaged friendship or relationship. In order to achieve this, the person must commence the projection of of a thought pattern of *'Light'* with one of *'Unconditional Love'* directed toward anyone who may nurture a grievance over past words or actions.

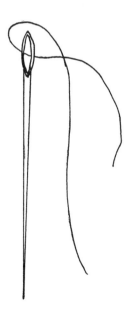

This symbol is often given to those who desire to

progress spiritually, and should they refuse to under
take this necessary action, they may discover that
those they have offended in the past, will re-enter
their lives at a critical point in their development,
and become an obstacle

The Oak Tree symbol-
ises strength, courage,
and protection. It also
reflects the influence
of the planet Mars in
the Nature Kingdom.
It indicates a strong,
protective nature.

An Octopus serves as
a clear indication of a
very difficult situation
ahead and of the need
to deal with an extrem-
ely possessive individ-
ual. It represents a maj-
or test or initiation and
you should bear in
mind that the true init-
iate overcomes such
situations by accepting
the necessity for them.

An **Olive Branch** is
relatively simple to
translate, for it indica-
tes an offer of peace
from a former adver-
sary which you would
be well advised to
accept.

To be shown **An Orange,** first whole and then segmented, indicates the need for compassion, and to open up, sharing all of the various aspects (or segments) of your nature with others.

In Atlantis **The Orange Tree** was considered to be sacred for its fruit represented the Planetary Overseer (known to us as Adam.) The orange (rather than the apple) was therefore the forbidden fruit).

The Owl - see under Birds.

Pansies - see under flowers

A Parrot is really a warning not to gossip without giving due thought and consideration to the nature of the information and the consequences of such acts. It can also indicate the need to ponder deeply upon knowledge gleaned from various sources, to ensure that you have a full understanding of it before sharing this with others.

The Path (where its end is hidden from view). This represents the spiritual path that lies ahead of you. As this has no end in sight and much of what is to transpire upon it is obscured from view, the spiritua aspirant will need much courage in order to complete the journey that lies ahead. Where

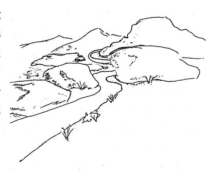

obstacles or difficulties are indicated along the way translate these accordingly, illustrating them for what they are - necessary impediments to aid the attainment of a spiritual goal.

The Peacock - see under birds.

The Phoenix rising from the ashes represents a form of rebirth or spiritual renewal. The indication being that you should now be prepared to soar to new heights, with the conflicts of the past behind you.

Pine Trees are symbolic of healing energies and can be translated in several ways; either you are in need of healing, or possess healing potential. Equally, this symbol can represent a need to become involved in or associated with a healing undertaking.

A Pomegranate is another of those fruits revered by the ancients for it was considered to be the sacred fruit of Osiris / Isis, the Divine Rulers of ancient Egypt. Where this is shown it serves to indicate an association with these evolved beings, formed during an earlier incarnation.

A Pool of Water (in the midst of a forest glade) symbolises the need for stillness within the self in order to gain a true reflection of your inner purpose. This is often a plea to commence meditation exercises in a bid to expand self awareness.

A Small Leather Pouch from which silver or gold coins tumble, represent benefits which will flow once you complete a specific task. If coloured gems pour from the pouch, they represent spiritual qualities or talents that await activation. The colour of the gems reflecting the nature of those talents. (See chapter 5)

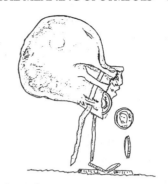

A **Precipice** is a clear warning that you can proceed no further with a particular undertaking. Any attempt to do so will certainly result in disaster. It is time to take stock of life and to ponder the future. This symbol may also represent a challenge - to step 'into the void' and then find a pathway to higher purpose.

A **Procession** of people from another point in time, rallying behind a cross held aloft, indicates that a force of spirit helpers are making their way toward someone who has recently undergone a measure of spiritual awakening. They rally to the cause in a bid to aid the expansion of awareness within this individual.

A **Pyramid** is an ancient representation of a need for equilibrium, indicating a challenge for the spiritual aspirant who must now endeavour to develop a balanced outlook upon life. It also serves to indicate someone, who in their long-gone past

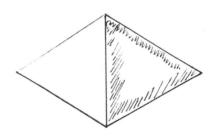

experienced a disciplined training within a mystery school in ancient Egypt (identified by the pyramid). This is a clear instruction to the aspirant - seek deep within the subconscious mind for that which lies hidden therein.

Where the image of the pyramid appears in the midst of a deep violet light it is an indication that occult truth and awareness may be reactivated once more, through the attainment of a balanced outlook on life coupled with diligent research. A pyramid also represents the **Master Builder** - someone who has incarnated once again in a bid to master the numeric vibration of Twenty-two. (see chapter 6)

A Pyramid of Amethyst Hue is a clear indication of past endeavours within Temple Beautiful. Here the acolyte was instructed in all of the healing arts as we know them today. In addition all were taught how to utilise quartz crystals and gemstones to effect healing of the body. This training also incorporated the study of colour, sound and dance, all of which were considered to be efficacious and having a part to play in the effecting of a cure.

A Quill and Parchment represents a request from the spirit realm to begin to set down all knowledge acquired to date in order that others may benefit. It also symbolises the role ahead of you - to become the scribe or intuitive channel for higher minds.

The Rainbow is an extremely positive symbol, one which is often given when you have accepted the necessity for a dark or difficult phase in life. It is a confirmation from your spirit helpers that a promise made will be honoured. A symbol of hope.

The Ram - with horns lowered, indicates that a challenge lies ahead, (possibly from an Aries subject) who may well consider that you are encroaching on their territory.

The Raven - see under birds.

To see **Reins** attached to someone indicates that their Higher Self is endeavouring to control the Lower Will via some form of irksome, but necessary restraint. This symbol can also indicate the need to bring your thought patterns or ambition under control.

Rings represent the need to forge closer links with others and may possibly be an indication that a romantic relationship lies ahead.

The Rock is an ancient symbol representing the Father / Mother God, indicating that the aspirant must become rocklike in faith and be equally determined to overcome all obstacles encountered on the path toward your goal.

A Rose is closely associated with the expression of love and when shown this symbol you should always take very careful note of its colour, for this serves to indicate the nature of the loving link.

A Red Rose represents an earthly love, the communication coming from someone who has departed the Earth Plane, but with whom there is still a powerful link of love. This comes to assure those who may be grieving that their love still endures.

A Pink Rose denotes love of an unconditional nature, invariably brought by one of the spirit helpers who perceives the need for loving support, particularly after a rather trying initiation.

A Yellow Rose on the other hands denotes a link of minds, coming from a spirit teacher applauding a student who has progressed rather well.

A White Rose (devoid of thorns) is a rather special symbol for in Atlantis this was considered sacred, representing the feminine aspect of the Planetary Overseer - the being we refer to today as Eve.

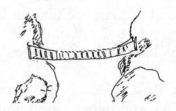

A Rope Bridge linking two sides of a gorge indicates that a major obstacle to further progress may now be overcome, but this will require steady nerves and great determination if the goal is to be attained.

Rough Seas are an indication of public opinion with regard to your ideals or undertakings. (This symbol can also reflect the opposition of friends or relatives) You have no option, other than to patiently ride out the storm.

A Rowing Boat with oars at the ready, riding upon the waves at the waters' edge is a clear signal that it is time to give serious thought to the task of rowing out into deeper waters and leaving your present environment (or outlook) behind.

Scales can have a dual meaning, either representing a deep desire for justice or the necessity to bring about a measure of equilibrium in your life.

The Sceptre symbolises authority, and to be given this staff of power indicates that great responsibility is soon to be placed upon your shoulders

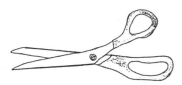

Scissors indicate the need to cut yourself free from a tie, either a relationship, a belief system, or a way of life upon which you have become too dependant and which is

now obstructing growth.

The Scorpion, its tail raised and moving swiftly toward you is a timely warning to move swiftly if you wish to avoid attack. It represents a vengeful individual whom you may have slighted in some manner. This is a foe for life.

The Seashore represents the need to extend your spiritual horizons and to be prepared to cross deep waters in order to achieve a desired goal.

The Serpent is yet another sacred symbol and, whereas we in the West tend to recoil from such creatures, in the East they have always symbolised divinity for they are considered to be the Guardians of Spiritual Truth on this, the earthly plane.

This is primarily a cosmic symbol, one which represents the energising, creative force of the spirit, known as the Kundalini Fire. It is a three pronged force and it is folly to strive to activate this until you have acquired the necessary measure of wisdom. The symbol is often presented as a timely warning - ignore it at your peril. In ancient Egypt it served to identify the initiate, and the acquisition of hidden or sacred knowledge.

A **Shark** circling just offshore is a clear warning that a predator lies in wait for those who plunge into the spiritual depths without the benefit of survival skills.

Sheaves of Corn represent spiritual harvest gathered in. This is usually given to someone who has, through exceptional effort, reaped a harvest of spiritual plentitude. The fruits of this harvest must now be stored and subsequently planted within the minds of those who seek truth.

A **Shepherd's Crook** symbolises the role ahead of you - to guard and protect the Creator's flock from attack by predators. An extremely responsible role, one often fulfilled as a teacher of esoteric subjects.

A **Shield** is an indication of the need to be prepared to defend yourself or your faith. If a cross or an emblem is emblazoned upon it, this represents the necessity to clearly identify yourself and your beliefs to those who oppose you.

A **Ship** adrift in stormy seas forewarns of a period of great difficulty ahead with the opinion

of others opposing personal actions or beliefs.   Be prepared to
ride out the storm.

A Sock hanging loose about the ankles is a clear indication that the individual concerned must now make a determined effort to play their part to the full within a particular undertaking or situation; in other words - 'pull up their socks. . . '

A Shoe or Shoes, often new and glamorous is a symbol which indicates that it is time to step out into something new.

A Skeleton. Although alarming to some, this really is quite a positive symbol for it depicts the end of one way of life and the commencement of another.

A Square is an interesting symbol for it depicts that which is without end - ie: a task that appears to be endless, or a relationship or belief system from which there is no escape.

Should you be given the symbol of **The   Sphynx,** which is half man half animal, it represents the necessity to control the lower nature if you are to be successful in your bid for self mastery. As the desire nature is extremely powerful, this will always be a difficult task to fulfill.   Little of real value can be attained until it is done.

A Spider within a web
represents danger lurk-
ing in the background
for   the unwary.   This
comes as a warning for

those who are spreading their wings spiritually, unaware that dark forces have them under observation.

The symbol of the **Star** is a very simple representation of light and indicates a need to reflect the measure of truth you have discovered to date. Take care to note the number of points on the star, for they serve to illustrate the manner in which you are to share the light of truth with mankind.

A **Four Pointed Star** indicates the necessity to be very practical and down to earth in your approach when attempting to share your concept of truth with others.

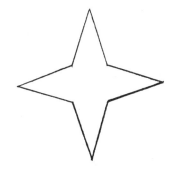

The **Five Pointed Star** is a symbol which represents man incarnate in the Plane of Matter, it also indicates someone who has reached the point of spiritual awakening. Five is a number which denotes the possession of powerful mental energies, and those for whom this symbol is received have the potential to become great communicators.

A **Six Pointed Star** represents someone who has incarnated to follow the mystical path. These individuals will need to activate the Heart Chakra, and to

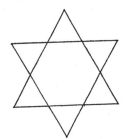

express a love for mankind which is free of all conditions . This is rarely a simple undertaking and
those who succeed could be said to be following in
the steps of the Christed Ones.   (See Chapter 6)

Star Within a Circle. This was the Circlet of Power
worn by the initiate priests of ancient civilisations.
It may indicate that assistance is being offered by a
spirit teacher who once held such a position or, alternatively, it illustrates the goal which the person concerned must strive to attain - ie: self mastery.

A Steam Train puffing up an incline, represents an
ability to take those who cling to an outmoded way
of life or belief system, toward a higher or greater
outlook on life. This may well prove to be an uphill
task at times, and a great deal of determination and
energy will be required, but this person has these
qualities in abundance.

Stepping Stones set within the bed of a stream illustrate a somewhat difficult period ahead, one where
you will have to carefully negotiate a precarious
path through the flow of astral or psychic energies
which lie before you - powerful forces which can so
very easily overwhelm the unwary.

Steps, either cut into a
cliff face or leading up
toward a building indi-
cate that the way ahead
may be steep, but that
assistance will be prov-
ided every step of the
way.

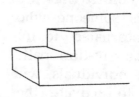

The Swastika is a very ancient symbol representing the combined energies of the cross and the circle. It is therefore a very potent sign, indicative of action.

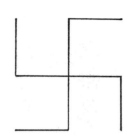

There are many meanings attached to it, although the majority of people still associate this with the dark forces unleashed by Adolph Hitler who reversed the swastika and abused its cosmic energies. It is considered to be symbolic of the creative forces within the Kingdom of Nature and is also referred to as The Hermetic Cross.

The Sword. This represents the Sword of Truth with which you may triumph over darkness and ignorance replacing these with the light of knowledge.

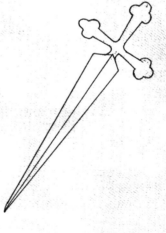

In order to progress, seekers of truth must always be prepared to fight for that which they perceive to be right, endeavouring to free those whose minds are bound by blind superstition and fear. Also bear in mind the fact that the tongue can be said to be a two-edged sword and that this symbol may also be taken as a warning relating to the abuse of speech.

The Tau. This is a variation of the cross, but here the upper segment of the cross is missing. It is considered to be a sacred symbol representing wisdom and learning. It is often seen with a serpent wound about it, representing the guardian of spiritual truth and mastery of the the lower nature.

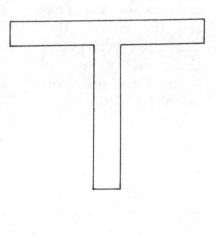

The Tiger is another symbol which forewarns of danger. Where the tiger watches intently, and is poised to attack this is a clear signal for you to leave a particular environment as swiftly and unobtrusively as possible. Should the tiger be leaping toward you, it may be a little late and you will now have to defend yourself as best you can. In itself the tiger represents a ferocious antagonist.

A Blazing Torch represents a service of enlightenment that lies ahead. It is associated with a former life in which you had been a bearer of the light of truth, particularly in Atlantis. It signifies the

necessity to become the light bearer (or torch bearer) once again a role that carries great personal responsibility.

Totem Poles indicate the presence of a spirit helper from a tribe of North American Indians, usually a former medicine man who comes to instruct in the art of healing.

A **Tower** attached to either a church or temple signifies the necessity to raise your level of consciousness, the way made relatively easy by the steps within the tower

Treasure recently unearthed or shown within a partially open casket illustrates good fortune ahead, repayment for tasks undertaken on behalf of others.

A **Tree** represents the need for growth and development, if you are to play your part as a protector of the lost or the weak. Should this be an oak tree it indicates the necessity to harness your Martian energy, utilising this to defend others when the need arises.

A **Triangle** within which a **Crucified Being** hangs on a **Cross,** is a major symbol which reveals that a form of self crucifixion lies ahead. If the cross is fixed to the upper portion of the triangle it is the Higher Self which must undergo a test, but where it is at a lower level, then it is the Lower Self or personality which must undergo crucifixion.

To be taken into **a Tunnel** symbolises the commencement of a dark phase in life, one wherein all outside help or direction will be blocked from view. During this period it would be advisable to keep your thoughts on track and press on regardless. If a dim light can be seen at the far end of the tunnel, it indicates that this difficult phase of life may be short lived.

An Umbrella held open above your head, indicates protection being offered in the face of adversity. This may be unexpectedly offered by an associate, or come from a spirit helper. Should there be light streaming from beneath the umbrella, it suggests that with this protection comes enlightenment.

A Unicorn represents the need to be in total control of all thought output and to activate and utilise the clairvoyant faculty (represented by the horn) using this to pierce the veil of ignorance and guide others toward their spiritual purpose.

A Grape Vine is a symbol with deep occult meaning. It is said that the vine originally bore only purple fruit, which represented the Divine Twins. Arbal and Arbel Jesus, who were part of the group of non-physical over-seers, sent to aid the development of the Animal Kingdom on Earth.

After the masculine aspect fell in Lemuria (as Cain) they divided into two seperate entities and the vine began to bear green grapes as well as the purple. The green grape represents the feminine aspect which incarnated as the World Teacher for the Age of Pisces, Jesus of Nazareth.

The old saying "By their fruits shall ye know them" is reflected here and anyone given the symbol of the green grapes are those who are drawn to the light of the Piscean Master and who may in turn receive guidance and direction from this Master Soul when they are perceived to be worthy of this. The purple grapes of course, reflect the energy of the masculine aspect of the Divine Twins, which has a major role to play in the expansion of human consciousness during the Aquarian Age.

A Violin (or a Violinist) is a symbol reflecting a latent ability for Trance Mediumship. This may prove to be a difficult undertaking - the training for which includes a great deal of study. There are certain health risks attached to this form of mediumship and these should not be lightly dismissed. (See Chapter 8)

Volcanoes represent a destructive or volatile personality creating havoc within its environment. **The Smoking Volcano** is a warning that the emotional nature must be brought firmly under control.

This symbol is often associated with relationships. Where a **Fiery Volcano** is shown it indicates the destruction of a current situation. It also represents a stern warning on the necessity to control emotional outbursts.

Water has several meanings, for it can represent the spiritual depths which must be plumbed, or astral forces that are preventing further growth. For many people water relates to the power of their emotional nature which must be mastered. The sensitive must take careful note of how the image is presented and translate this accordingly.

Where a **Waterfall** is shown crashing from on high into a pool far below, it serves to illustrate powerful spiritual forces that are about to be channelled into your life. The unwary may be overwhelmed by this sudden inrush of spiritual energies, and this symbol should be seen as a forewarning of a need to be ever watchful and to maintain strict control over mental and emotional expression.

A **Waterlily** with an **Eye** at its centre represents the feminine asppect of the Creative Being - or **The Mother God** and the need to serve Her Will by activating and utilising, the sensitive or feminine aspect of our dual

nature.

A **Wild Boar** running amok is an ancient symbol indicating that the lower nature is out of control - creating havoc within the immediate environment, and that steps should be taken to rectify this.

The Wilderness. Where a barren wilderness is shown, strewn with rocks and boulders, it reflects a difficult period ahead which must be endured, in order to overcome the test that it represents. With determination and courage, the individual can succeed.

An Open Window represents the ability to look beyond your current environment and the restrictions it places upon you and perceive that which lies on the far horizon. This comes as a message of hope for anyone who feels trapped in their present environment. Should the window be closed, it indicates the necessity to stimulate the clairvoyant faculty, acquiring thereby, a measure of awareness of future events.

Winged Sandals relate to potent Mercurial energies which can be called upon in a bid to bring about an expansion of consciousness. This symbol can also identify someone who is a natural communicator.

A Yacht upon rough seas indicates the ability to sail close to the wind, and to readily adapt to ever changing situations, whilst sear-

ching for new spiritual
horizons.

Symbols are a simple picture language which is
easily translatable. Look for the most obvious meaning and if in doubt ask your communicators for
confirmation. Do also remember that you may always *question* those who seek to communicate
with you. Where your link is indeed with the teachers of the higher sub-plane of the Mental Plane,
clear answers will always be provided.

CHAPTER FIVE

THE OCCULT POWERS OF GEMSTONES

As spiritual aspirants begin to expand their clairvoyant faculty it will soon become evident that their basic knowledge of symbolism is no longer sufficient, their spiritual horizons being constantly extended by their spirit inspirers with the transmission of images of a deeply occult nature. This is to ensure that channels continue to expand their level of awareness and to test their ability to translate the images presented to them.

Quite often these images will depict cups, swords or crowns, all heavily embellished with precious gems, and the sensitive will then need to acquire knowledge of the occult significance of each gemstone.

Aquamarine is *The Seers Stone* (or magicians stone) one greatly prized by the ancients, (although they preferred the Beryl which is much the same.) Where this jewel is presented, or is set in a ring or a cup etc, it indicates that you have the capacity for seership and that this gem should be utilised in a bid to stimulate this ability.

The **Amethyst** is *The* initiates stone, for through-out time it has served to identify the disciplined being, someone who has in their past, entered the mystery school, and mastered self therein. In Atlantis, this was set in a small silver or golden disc, worn over the brow chakra, whilst the Initiate Priests had this set in the golden band they wore around the forehead.

This gem possesses no 'occult' value whatsoever if purchased for the self but, if following a traumatic period in life a person is presented with an Ame-thyst gemstone, it is a clear signal from 'on high', that they have passed a major initiation.

Crystals: To have quartz crystals placed before you or to be shown a number of these, is a clear intima-tion that there is a need to work with crystals on a daily basis, in a bid to expand your level of consc-iousness, either in the field of seership, or in some form of healing undertaking.

Where a ring or sword is adorned with a **Diamond,** it indicates a need for courage in an undertaking that lies ahead, and for you to endeavour to acquire a measure of mental or emotional clarity compar-able with that of the diamond. It can also represent the need for cunning when dealing with a powerful adversary. In former times soldiers often wore a dia-mond on their sword arm and when this caught the the sun's rays, the reflection served to blind their opponent.

The Emerald is another gemstone which is related to initiation. In this case it serves to illustrate the many disciplines which await you within the area of the healing arts, for this is the *Initiates Stone of Healing*. Where this is shown in any manner, be it upon a ring, cup, sword etc, it reflects powerful healing potential which must first be activated and taken to its greatest level of expression.

If the Emerald adorns a ring, then the indication is that a committment or dedication of the self to the art of healing has to be made. Should it adorn the hilt of a sword, then you must be prepared to attack ignorance, or to defend those who serve in healing-related undertakings. Where the Emerald decorates a cup or challice, it illustrates the need to become a healing vessel.

Lapis Lazuli was much prized by the ancients, particularly the Egyptians, and it is often termed 'The Sapphire of the Ancients'. It is a very powerful gem which serves to activate the chakras, particularly when worn upon the breast. Where this stone is highlighted in some manner it indicates the possession of mediumistic talents, and that this jewel will assist in their stimulation, when worn above the diaphragm.

The Moonstone is closely associated with the Moon and, in turn, with all forms of mediumistic expression. It is said to possess a particular ability to enable a sensitive to observe the auric patterns of the enquirer.

The Opal is also known as *The Eye Stone* , as it was

used by the ancients to treat disorders of the eye.   If shown this stone set in a ring or pendant, it could represent a warning referring to a changeable or insincere person, or the necessity to be less changeable in your own outlook.

Pearls represent wisdom and where these are seen decorating clothing, or rings etc, or should you be presented with a single pearl, or a string of pearls, it signifies the pursuit of wisdom. Having acquired a measure of wisdom you must not, in your enthusiasm, thrust this on those who are not ready to embrace it, heeding the biblical warning "cast ye not pearls before swine."

The Ruby is a gem which is said to possess the ability to forewarn its wearer of any danger that lies ahead. This it achieves by becoming cloudy and dull. It is said that Catharine of Aragon was forewarned of her fate in this way. This is a very material gem, and relates to greed and desire - hence the tales about unlucky rubies.

The deep blue **Sapphire** is yet another gem which identifies the disciplined being, or initiate. It is closely associated with the Druidic priesthood of the past, who utilised this gem to denote those who had mastered their thought processes, becoming thereby, Initiates. Where a deep blue sapphire is offered to you or decorates any symbolic item such as a ring or cup, it is a clear indication that mastery of their runaway thought patterns is absolutely necessary, if they are to achieve any measure of success in life.

Whenever you perceive gemstones, take careful note of the size and the variety of the gems themselves, together with the style of the item they adorn and the various embellishments thereon, for they all relate to the past attainments of the person concerned, and should be described in a clear manner.

CHAPTER SIX

NUMERIC FACTORS

In an earlier chapter, I pointed out the necessity to take careful note of the number of points on a star or whether you'see' one or two objects in a clairvoyant image. To overlook these pointers is to fail to tranlate the communication correctly. The seer should therefore acquire a basic understanding of numerology.

No. 1. Relates to leadership, masculinity, independence, and the need to lead others by the power of example - never through domination or by the strength of the will. It is also important to note that failure can also come about by refusing to accept responsibility, or by becoming a clinging vine.

No. 2: Regardless of whether one is male or female, this number represents the feminine aspect of our dual nature, that portion of the self which is aware of the Will of The Creator. Where two of anything is shown, the indication is that in order to succeed with whatever this represents, you must utilise your intuitive or clairvoyant abilities within the situation or undertaking. For example, two flowers indicate a potential for spiritual blossoming - provided that the mediumistic qualities are utilised. Equally, this number also indicates that the emotional nature will have to be mastered if you are to achieve any measure of success in life.

No. 3: This indicates the need for self expression, expansion and growth, during the current life experience, which can be achieved via the development of an artistic or creative ability. The greatest obstacle to success however may lie in the tendency to procrastinate, whilst social events may receive too much attention.

No. 4: This number illustrates the possession of a strong will which must be disciplined and used constructively at at all times. It also reflects the need to develop a practical and down to earth approach toward any undertaking. Resentment of those in authority and a tendency to rebel against the established order of the day may well lead to failure.

No. 5: This vibration reflects the possession of powerful mental abilities, and the necessity to learn how to utilise these in a constructive manner.This number indicates the potential teacher or communicator, but the negative aspect of this vibration may lead to all manner of backsliding, abuse of thought, and the pursuit of illusionary pastimes.

No. 6: Wherever the six vibration is evident, ie: as six petals or leaves upon a flower, or points on a star, it signifies a task that must be undertaken in the spirit of unconditional love, with the need to activ-

ate the Heart Chakra. This can prove to be a very trying vibration to master, for until you fully compre-
hend the enormity of this particular lesson, you
may spend much time in search of love, and become extremely possessive of those whom you
claim to love. Long term commitment to any relationship may also prove to be difficult.

No. 7: Of all the numeric factors, this is perhaps the
most important, for it clearly identifies the natural
medium and the need to follow the mystical path
throughout life. It also indicates an extremely sensitive nature and possibly a fearful personality. Encourage such individuals to overcome their irrational
fears (of the unknown) and to express their latent
talents.

No. 8: A numeric vibration which has a powerful
Saturnian influence the number eight, wherever it
appears, will serve to continually test you throughout your lifetime and, until you learn to patiently
accept the inevitable, life may prove to be extremely
difficult. In addition, the number eight encourages
the pursuit of monetary gain, coupled with a desire
to control the lives of others. At its highest level,
this number can produce the potential initiate .

No. 9: This number identifies a caring nature, and
clearly illustrates the pathway you should follow
throughout life. In order to find true satisfaction you
will need to pursue a service-oriented career, but
must learn to control your Martian temperament.
This is a vibration which indicates the necessity for
the completion of an undertaking commenced during an earlier incarnation.

No. 11.   Serves to identify the idealist and the dreamer. You have to learn to keep your feet firmly planted upon terra firma, seeking a practical method of expressing your ideals in everyday life. Failure to do so can lead to a deal of rejection and loneliness. (Deeds not words might prove to be the best advice for such individuals). Life may be made even more difficult by your reluctance to change your mind once a decision has been reached.

No. 22:   An extremely difficult numeric vibration to master, for it indicates the necessity to remain calm, cool, and collected at all times, whilst demonstrating a totally balanced point of view to the world at large. Strong humanitarian traits manifest with this vibration.

Those who wish to pursue this fascinating subject further may find my earlier work ' Master Your Vibration' thought provoking.

CHAPTER SEVEN

THE HUMAN AURA

As the clairvoyant faculty expands the sensitive will begin to perceive the aura of those who come in search of truth and spiritual direction, and the correct translation of that which they then observe is extremely important.

Surrounding the physical form are a series of 'subtle bodies' which are collectively referred to as the aura, due to their colourful radiance.   Each of these non-physical forms has a part to play in the life experience of the individual, and each in turn tells the clairvoyant much about the person concerned.

In order of appearance these are the Etheric Body: Emotional Body: and the Mental Body.

The Etheric Body immediately surrounds the human form and is composed of electromagnetic particles.   It extends some three to five centimetres beyond the physical form of most people. The more evolved the person is, the wider this subtle-body will be, and around certain individuals it can extend some fifteen centimetres beyond their physical form.

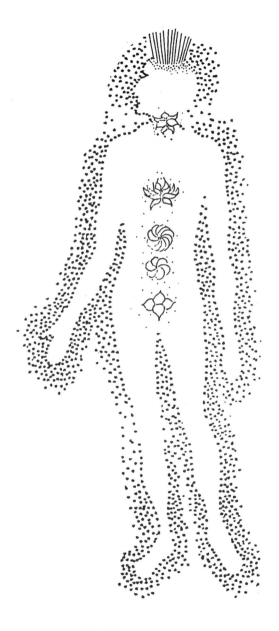

**The Etheric Body
and The Major Chakras**

As the atoms of this outer energy-field inter-penetrate the earthly form, it tends to mirror its contours and is often referred to as the Etheric Double. It is an essential part of the life support system, sustaining the physical body with a form of energy known as 'Prana'. This energy it obtains from sunlight and the various colour rays that flow through the ethers, absorbing these via the seven major chakras, a series of vortices which are located within the Etheric Body.

Invariably, this non-physical replica has a creamy-white hue. However, where a person has been subject to a great deal of restraint over a period of time, it can result in a sense of frustration or a deep-seated resentment. This negative response to such events will eventually be reflected in an unpleasant shade of grey-green within the Etheric Body. Unless that person is prepared to accept the situation as it is, or to discipline their emotional responses to such events, they may well develop a rather painful health condition, such as rheumatoid or osteo-arthritis.

Many caring people spend part of their day consciously projecting loving thoughts towards those who are sick, or spend a deal of time in prayer on behalf of the afflicted. In response to this constructive use of the power of thought, their Etheric Body expands considerably, often extending to some fifteen centimetres beyond their physical form.

Their Etheric Body then becomes extremely radiant, reflecting thoughts of ' *light* ' which they have projected towards others and this in turn illumines the whole of their aura. As a result many people are then drawn toward them,the light within their aura acting as a magnet.

Some schools of thought describe the second of our 'subtle bodies' as the Emotional Body whilst others refer to it as the Astral Body, largely because it is composed of seven grades of astral matter. This has its seat in the Sacral Chakra, (the seat of the lower nature), and can vary in size according to the evolution of the person concerned.

This subtle body has its origin within the desires of human nature, reflecting our everyday emotional thought patterns or physical desires, and surrounds both the physical and etheric forms. Around the less evolved members of the human race (who often fall prey to all manner of lower desires) their Emotional Body may only extend for some twenty-five centimetres beyond their etheric form, but around the majority of mankind, this body is usually some forty-five centimetres wide.With a spiritually awakened (and active) person, it tends to be far more extensive and luminous.

Where a person is deeply enmeshed in expression of the lower senses, their Emotional Body will reflect this activity in murky shades of colour drawn from the lower part of the spectrum, such as dark reds, muddy browns and heavy greys. Emotional activity of a more positive nature, such as caring and compassionate acts, undertaken in the spirit of selfless love, will result in colours of a much more positive nature, such as clear orange or rose pink and a greater luminosity throughout the aura.

The third of our subtle forms is termed the Mental

Etheric Body

Emotional Body

Mental Body

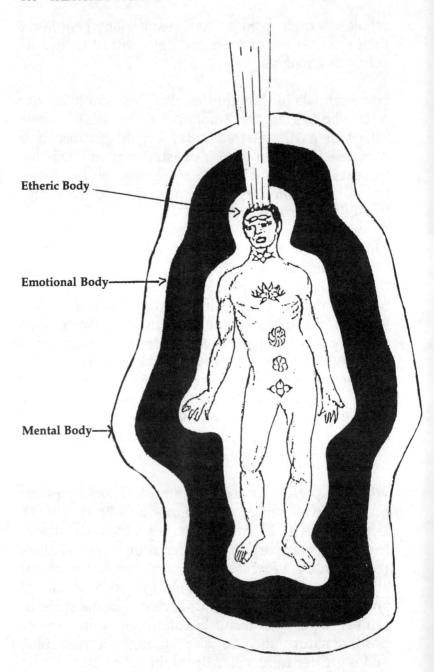

The third of our subtle forms is termed the Mental Body, through which the Higher Self finds expression and this subtle body has two quite seperate aspects, each fulfilling totally different roles. The lower of these reflects those thought patterns which arise within the conscious mind, whilst the upper aspect corresponds with the principles of the higher mind and this portion is known as the Causal Body.

Where we endeavour to expand our mental faculties, the lower portion of the Mental Body will be bright, shining and usually golden yellow in hue. This is particularly true of those with a highly developed intellect. However, should we abuse the power of our mind, and sink into states of depravity, then the sensitive will note areas of darkness in the lower portion of the Mental Body.

The higher segment of the Mental Body is invariably green in its colouring, and indicates the possession of a metally creative capacity, one which should be channelled into creative undertakings, such as the arts or literature.

Beyond the Mental Body are recorded skills or qualities of the Spirit Self, abilities developed through self-discipline in former life experiences. These skills - often referred to as 'spiritual gifts' are those which set an individual apart from others, and the seer should encourage this person to reactivate these dormant qualities, for they will aid in successfully attaining personal destiny.

The shades of colour observed within the aura have specific meanings, as do those perceived around symbolic images during the early stages of spiritual unfoldment. In common with the science of numbers, once seers are able to recognise the form of energy represented by each colour, they may then then readily translate this for those drawn to them in their hour of need.

Dark Red within the aura is a reflection of a deeply emotional and - at times - a highly sensual nature. Those with a deal of this colour visible in their emotional body tend to experience life through the physical senses.

Tomato Red (orange overtones) indicates the awakening of the caring aspect of the nature, but nonetheless, this person is still highly emotional and quite materialistic in outlook.

Scarlet is often the reflection of suppressed anger. This colourful response within the aura then serves to repel all other individuals.

Crimson indicates the possessive individual (possibly a parent or lover,) but it also serves to indicate those who become possessed by their worldly wealth and possessions.

Rose Pink is the purest aspect of the Red Ray, and it reflects the ability to share love in an unconditional manner. It indicates an unselfish person who exacts no return for that which they give to others.

Orange (clear and bright) indicates a compassionate individual, someone with a deeply caring nature, often given to charitable undertakings.

Orange (dark and murky) is a reflection of pride and ambition. As these characteristics can so often mar the lifetime, advance warning should be given to the person concerned, but the advice may well be rejected out of hand. Quite often this shade of orange also indicates a measure of imbalance within the Sacral Chakra.

Primrose Yellow reveals an artistic nature and the person should be encouraged to express this through some form of creative activity. This colour can also denote the intellectual who devotes a deal of time to the investigation of spiritual matters and will be noted in the Mental Body by the sensitive.

Golden Yellow indicates the teacher, or someone who is possessed of a powerful ability to communiicate, a quality which should be channelled into the arts, theatre, dance, or the media. Once again, this colour will be noted in the Mental Body.

Ochre (yellow/orange). Should this rather unpleasant shade of colour be observed in the Emotional Body, the sensitive should warn of the danger attached to a tendency to utilise the intellect in a highly selfish manner. Should people choose to ignore the warning, they may well reap a bitter harvest in the fullness of time.

Gold represents the philosopher or the mathematician, those who utilise their intellect in the most positive manner. Once again, this particular shade of colour will be noted by the sensitive in the Mental

Body.

Lime Green indicates those who endeavour to express At-One-ment with the Creator, harmonious and balanced in views and outlook upon life.

Grey / Green. This unpleasant shade reflects long-term resentment or frustration. It can also serve to identify a deceitful or sly nature and will be noted in the Emotional Body.

Emerald Green indicates a harmonious individual, someone who is extremely resourceful and versatile and possessed of a powerful imagination. The peace maker.

Dark Green usually represents a deal of restlessness or impatience within the self, identifying an individual who longs for change. This colour is invariably noted in the lower segment of the Emotional Body.

Turquoise identifies a person who is extremely adaptable, possessing a very sympathic nature.

Light Blue reflects the spiritual nature indicating someone who is extremely sensitive and quite psychic. Noted in the outer aura, beyond the Causal Body.

Royal Blue can reflect the religious outlook of an individual or alternatively, it serves to indicate the possession of a strong intuitive ability; a quality which can be utilised to bypass the astral planes when in search of truth. . . A quality of the Higher Self.

Violet is an indication of the initiate of yesteryear and the subconscious possession of a deal of occult knowledge. A person with great inner strength with the ability to overcome all obstacles.

Amethyst is the purest aspect of the Violet Ray and where this colour appears within the aura, it reflects the possession of a natural healing ability - a talent that should be determinedly reactivated during the current lifetime. As this is the *greatest* of the spiritual qualities, it is an ability to cherish, and one that should be given particular attention.

Radiance throughout the aura represents the ability of the person to bring enlightenment and upliftment to others on many different levels. It signifies a joyful, a cheerful person.

CHAPTER EIGHT

KARMA
And INITIATION

Throughout this book I constantly refer to initiation and karma and perhaps it would be as well at this point to clarify just what I mean by these words.

Karma is a Sanscrit word meaning repayment. In other words - that which we do unto others will, in the fullness of time, be visited upon us. Karma is also referred to as Cause and Effect or the Law of Sequence and Consequence, whilst the bible refers to it as 'an eye for an eye!'

This extremely just law takes various forms including Instant Karma (a form of restitution for unkind or unjust acts). Of all the forms which karma takes, this perhaps is the more acceptable, for at least we have awareness of our acts of injustice or wrong-doing.

Then there are those forms of suffering which it is our fate to undergo. The decision to repay these long-term debts is taken by our Over - Self (the Spiritual Reality) and the Lords of Karma prior to the current round of physical experience.

The Lower Will (or Ego) has no awareness of what lies before it, nor of the situations which have lead to this round of repayment. The Ego invariably considers the stressful and often painful experiences it must face in life as injustice on the part of The Creator yet, as I have already stated, this is the most just of laws.

In our past we have abused our Divine gift of Free Will, (perhaps by refusing to allow other people to exercise theirs) and must now, in consequence, make due repayment. This form of karma must be fully met during the current life experience and cannot be sidestepped, much as we may wish we could.

Many query what purpose this can possibly serve, if we have no awareness of the actions which lead to the round of repayment. Quite simply, such situations act as a necessary test or form of initiation and, depending upon our responses, we either grow spiritually by our acceptance of that which is patently inevitable, or fail by refusing to co-operate. The latter reaction may merely serve to exacerbate an already difficult situation.

Bear in mind that the true initiate is he or she who humbly accepts the necessity for such painful experiences, whilst the fool, by refusal to accept, merely extends their period of suffering.

In conclusion let me add that not all karma is unpleasant or related to difficulties, for there is good Karma to be reaped also. Positive acts undertaken in former lifetimes where we have offered a helping hand to others, supporting them in their hour of need, must also be repaid. As we progress through life we will encounter those 'familiars' once more and they will go out of their way to improve our lot in life. For as we sow, so shall we reap. . .

The purpose of incarnation into this Plane of Matter is to provide each individual soul with opportunities for growth. All is very carefully planned in advance. A blueprint (or pattern) for the life experience ahead is created by the Overself together with the Lords of Karma and once incarnate, the evolving soul will be inspired by Greater Minds to follow a particular pathway through life.

This entails the undergoing of a number of physical, emotional and mental challenges, each of which has a lesson to impart. These situations are known as Intiations. This term literally means purification and the experiences are intended to slowly awaken the soul to its true purpose.

There are Lesser Initiations - which are associated with the Four Seasons and the Elements of Earth, Air, Fire and Water. These lesser challenges may be experienced many times until the soul comes to accept the lessons each of these has to teach. For instance. The Water Initiation represents the purification of the soul and its preparation for other tests. This initiation is largely experienced by undergoing a series of emotional conflicts, whilst the Fire Initiation serves to stimulate a desire to love all of creation unconditionally.

The Greater Mysteries are seven year initiations - a

period wherein the now awakened soul endeavours to attain particular goals, ranging from the activation of the intuitive ability and seeking to become The Messenger of the Gods - to total self mastery under the Seventh Initiation.

Each and every one of us is a potential Master and the various stages of initiation, once successfully undertaken will, life after life, gradually lead us to that point of total self mastery which is after all, the whole purpose of incarnation into the Plane of Matter.

Our journey through matter is governed by certain spiritual laws which have a direct bearing upon our spiritual growth. These are The Law of Karma (which is *The Natural Law* - also referred to as Sequence and Consequence or the Law of Cause and Effect): The Law of Forgiveness (also termed Redemption), and The Law of Initiation. As I have already stated, where we inflict harm upon another or cause suffering in order to further selfish aims, we break that Natural Law and as a consequence create Karma.

When at some future point in'time' you are undergoing a painful repayment of a karmic debt, you may well become resentful of those who have brought this situation into being. However such thought patterns merely serve to exacerbate the problem. If you can detach yourself from the situation (difficult though that may be) and try to perceive the event as the outworking of a Greater Law, then you may soon resolve it.

This can be achieved by concentrating on the person(s) concerned and mentally projecting toward them a thought pattern of *'Light'*. Maintain this for several minutes before switching to a thought pattern of *'Love'*. (Initially this may b e a difficult undertaking, particularly if you harbour a deal of resentment against that individual.) Where this is the case direct a *Rose Pink Ray* from the region of your Heart Chakra in their direction, focussing this upon them for several minutes. Then send out the thought pattern *"I forgive you!"* This must of course be sincerely meant and not merely empty words.

If you can undertake this in a detached manner each and every day (several times a day if you so wish) then the matter will soon be resolved. "How?" you may ask! Again the answer lies with the Lords of Form.

Your thoughts of 'Light' and 'Unconditional Love' coupled with your forgiveness of that individual for their actions, are clearly noted in the ethers. In turn, this brings about the merging of the Law of Karma and the Law of Forgiveness - the outcome of which is the activation of The Law of Initiation. You then undergo an expansion of your level of consciousness. In this manner do we all progress toward self mastery.

CHAPTER NINE

FORMS OF MEDIUMSHIP

Mediumship is the ability to become both receiver and transmitter of information from the non-physical planes of consciousness. For those who are slowly awakening to the awareness that they possess such abilities there can be uncertainty as to which form their new-found talent should take, or which method of expression would be most suitable to them.

There are a great many avenues available to the developing sensitive. So many in fact that it often leads to a deal of confusion. The potential seer may at first elect to study one of the simpler forms of mediumship, making their selection from among tarot card reading, crystal ball gazing. For the more adventurous there could be psychometry, sand reading, flower clairscentience, or aura reading.

The choice is of course a matter of personal preference dependant to a degree, upon the form of mediumship the individual has witnessed to date and their current level of evolution. But each of these tools will enable sensitives to express their intuitive or clairvoyant talents according to ability.

No matter the object utilised in such undertakings, be it a ring or watch when demonstrating psychometry; a tray of sand; a flower; the tarot cards; or a crystal ball; all serve as reflectors of clairvoyant or intuitive ability. They should never be considered to be an end in themselves, for if this happens sensitives place limits upon their mediumistic skills

Indeed, true seers will constantly search for further opportunities to express and expand their mediumistic talent. They will be eager to move on when it becomes evident that they can achieve little of further benefit, for themselves or others, within the confines of their current form of expression.

Nonetheless, there are many mediums who, having reached a particular stage in their development, openly boast of their abilities and make the most astonishing claims with regard to their talents. All must bear in mind the fact that they are but the vessel for the various communications, and not their source. Spiritual pride is folly. It is a major pitfall that lies in wait for all who strive to serve mankind.

For so many, their first introduction to spirit communication comes at a party , when someone decides to play games. They set out letters in a circle upon a table together with the words 'yes' and 'no', in the centre of which an upturned glass is placed. Each of those gathered around the table then place one finger upon the glass, and then attempt to communicate with spirit entities.

this is usually undertaken in a frivolous way, few of those participating really believing that such contacts are possible.To their astonishment the glass often moves off at high speed, only ceasing its motion when it reaches a particular letter around the board. A burst of hilarity tinged with fear is the usual response to such activity, yet they continue the experiment, hiding their fear behind loud laughter.

None of the participants may realise that one among them possesses a latent mediumistic ability, a quality which is being stimulated in a bid to effect the link with the spirit communicants. This individual is, more often than not, blissfully unaware of of such dormant potential, little realising that this experiment has been set in motion by their spirit helpers, in a bid to awaken them to their personal destiny.

Communications of this nature are fraught with danger, for we have no means of testing the veracity of the statements made by the spirit communicators and, initially, all such comunications are innocuous and seemingly harmless. Problems arise when the sensitive begins to utilise this form of communication on a regular basis.

The spirit entity gradually begins to gain the confidence of those who seek for truth in this way, and quite often will claim to be a highly evolved being or a historical figure. And, at times a loved one.The information is usually accepted without question; and so the astral entity can thus gain control (perhaps with possession in mind.)

How is this possible? It is largely done through the the power of thought. When agreeing to participate in such experiments, individuals have a desire to obtain certain information, or to communicate with a specific entity. Their thought-forms are observed by those astral entities bent on mischief, and when the entities labouriously spell out the desired communication, the individual concerned is duly astonished and wants more. (This is the pitfall!!)

Such mischievous entities will continue to play on people's credulity and eventually the entities begin to assert authority, issuing all manner of commands. Within a short space of time the mind, and subsequently the life of the querent is no longer their own.

Many of those who regularly indulge in this dangerous pastime require long - term medical treatment. It is extremely sad to witness such events, but those who reject all advice to the contrary (and foolishly play with fire) must be prepared to get their fingers burned.

All who endeavour to communicate with the spirit realms need to learn to take protective measures and to avoid undertakings which are fraught with danger. The fact that a soul has passed to the higher side of life does not mean that it automatically becomes wise and all-knowing, or that it is given wings and a harp.

Where people have been greedy, selfish, or just downright unpleasant during their most recent life experience, they will retain that mode of thought until they become aware of how destructive they were and desire to make amends. They are often, the same individuals we would avoid during the course of everyday life and the seeker after truth should learn to exercise a similar measure of discernment, when beginning to communicate with the non-physical realms.

Over the years I have assisted many who became addicted to this particular form of spirit communication. From a schoolgirl anxious to contact her late mother (who had suicided) to a mother determined to establish contact with a much loved son. And so many many more.

The schoolgirl was someone I encountered during a holiday in Spain some years ago. She and her companion, in a highly nervous state, told me that they were afraid to return to their hotel room. Asking the reason why, this young lady told me that due to the unwanted attentions of the hotel manager, they were in the habit of locking the door once they had entered their room. That evening however the door had burst open and a force like a wind rushed into and around the room, causing them to flee.

I found this tale rather puzzling. "Tell me what you had been doing before the door burst open" I asked. Looking at each other apprehensively, the second girl said "We. . . had been trying to contact her mother. . . ". I now began to see the reason for the strange phenomena they had described. "Why would you wish to do that?" I asked - "and what were you using to do so?" They giggled rather nervously before replying. "A glass and some letters we wrote on pieces of paper. . . the girls at school do it often!"

"But tell me why you wish to contact your mother" I asked this distressed young girl. She shook her head, tears now pouring down her face. Finally her friend answered. "Her mom committed suicide - and she wants to know why!"

My spiritual knowledge was fairly limited at that stage in my life but I had been lead to believe that when someone committed suicide, that soul was then isolated on the Astral Plane and could not be contacted in any way. This information I shared with my distressed friends, advising them of the dangers attached to playing with forces they did not fully understand. I also offered to take them both to a reputable medium in London once my holiday was over, and this they agreed to.

Upon my return I booked into a group session with a trance medium whom I respected. During the course of the evening, her spirit 'control' brought forward the late mother of my young friend. She was extremely distressed and asked me to help her daughter who apparently, was also contemplating suicide. I was quite shaken by this information.

"But. . . I have have been told that you cannot contact those who commit suicide - and I have told her daughter this!" I exclaimed to the 'control'. To which he replied. "That was your awareness until this moment my son - we have now extended it."

The following evening I rang the girl and told her what had transpired - that her mother was happy in her new environment but concerned for her mental well being. "If you wish" I continued, "I can take you to this medium next week and perhaps your mother will come and speak to you!" There was a lengthy silence before she replied. "No - I don't think so. If mom is okay - then I will be too. Thanks for the help."

In this situation I, with my limited knowledge, was utilised in a bid to prevent yet another tragedy. Had I not been visiting the same town, who knows what would have happened.

In the majority of cases where people were prepared to step back from the brink, little harm was done. They were then encouraged to seek a safer form of communication. In other, more tragic situations, exorcism became necessary. My advice! Avoid this form of communication and seek the aid of a reputable medium.

The **Tarot cards** read by a psychic are for many people their introduction to spirit communication, although in most cases, these cards are merely used for fortune telling. The tarot read by a competent psychic can indeed provide a deal of personal direction, for the cards can clearly identify the way ahead for the querant. Much depends upon the intuitive ability of the psychics concerned, as to whether or not the cards can provide an accurate reading.

As the channel is dependant upon the inspiration they receive during such undertakings, it is very important that they ascertain where the source of their inspiration lies. There are a great many tarot packs available today, many accompanied by books on how to read them. The seeker who wishes to explore this field would be well advised to take the time to research the history of the designers of the various packs of cards. It needs to be understood that some designers of Tarot Cards are associated with dark forces. And channels who use such cards may then quite unwittingly, come under the influence of a dark force.

In the hands of a spiritually awakened channel the tarot can provide positive guidance on the spiritual path ahead (which is the purpose for which they were originally designed.) For the novice they can provide a powerful form of communication, whilst serving to focus attention upon the meaning of symbols. It is my personal opinion that the tarot cards can only be utilised as a stepping stone toward greater spiritual awareness.

The Crystal Ball has acquired a mystical reputation for aiding the perception of future events, yet in themselves, these spheres (the best of which are fashioned from the purest quartz crystal) serve merely as a reflective medium of the clairvoyant faculty of those who use them.

Where this ability is of the lower psychic variety, the the communications received will be extremely mundane, if not downright fanciful. A point all must bear in mind is that a crystal ball cannot stimulate abilities that one does not possess. But where any individual does have a dormant clairvoyant potential, frequent concentration upon a crystal ball could serve to activate this (provided that their clairvoyant ability is of the objective variety).

Clairvoyants can by and large, be divided into two categories. Those who 'see' objectively' - in other words, those who are able to observe two dimensions at one and the same time, ie: note what is taking place upon this Plane of Matter, whilst also observing the inhabitants of the Astral Realm which inter-penetrates it; and those who must close their eyes in order to obtain clairvoyant images.The latter are the subjective channels, and most sensitives come under this category.

Only the objective channels will gain benefit from the use of a crystal ball, whilst those who 'see' in a subjective manner would find that a clear quartz crystal would prove to be a greater catalyst. It would therefore be folly to expend a great deal of money on a crystal ball, which many do unthinkingly, when it may prove to be of little use.

The medium should also be aware of the unwritten law appertaining to the acquisition of a crystal ball. When a person is perceived to be ready to recommence their role as a seer, a Greater Mind will bring influence to bear upon a friend or relative who will then be impressed to give them a crystal ball.

Those who are impatient for growth or experience, and who by an act of will manifest things out of time, can in turn find themselves the tools of mischievous astral entities. Spiritual growth is by nature slow and the truly wise individuals are those who are content to make haste slowly.

Psychometry is often the first form of mediumistic expression for a great many sensitives, who find that by holding an article belonging to another person, and 'tuning-in' to the magnetic vibrations it carries, they gain a measure of insight into the emotional thought patterns and actions of that individual.

This of course is a psychic faculty, which utilises the Etheric Body (composed of electromagnetic particles) to 'tap-in' to those vibrations, and when they are correctly translated this psychic 'sensing' can provide an extremely accurate 'reading' of that person's recent activities.

Every single item that we wear or utilise during the course of our daily lives carries our personal magnetic vibration. The more frequently they are worn the clearer that energy imprint becomes. When endeavouring to translate such energy patterns, sensitives need to be aware that from the moment they begin to 'tune-in', every sensation they are then subject to relates to the enquirer.

The wise channel will not ignore a sudden, jabbing pain or pressure in the head as something appertaining to themselves (unless they happen to be prone to such attacks.) Invariably these painful sensations identify a health condition the enquirer is subject to and they should be advised of your findings.

During activity of this nature the channel becomes a highly sensitive 'receiving station' and needs to learn to share all that which is 'sensed' or 'felt' in a confident manner with the person concerned, for such information does have a part to play in the expansion of consciousness for both enquirer and channel. Psychometry is, however, a psychic undertaking and the channel desirous of advancing, will eventually endeavour to progress beyond the limitations it presents.

Nonetheless, every form of mediumship has a constructive aspect to it. Psychics who are called upon for assistance by police forces in various parts of the world are in part, using psychometery in the bid to trace missing persons.

By attuning to the energy pattern of the missing person via the items presented to them and following their intuitive ability they are often able to locate that missing individual. Such abilities are rare however, for the majority of psychometrists tend to be involuntary psychics - ie: they are unable to control their mediumistic abilities.

In contrast, mediums who have received a thorough and disciplined training can use a personal object worn by others to attune to their auras, enabling the channel to identify the spiritual abilities possessed by that person.

Similarly, articles can be used (with permission) to attune to their Akashic Record, assisting the sensitive to bring forward aspects of former lives, the attainments of which have a direct bearing on the role to be played in the current incarnation. A finely attuned medium may also utilise that object in a bid to provide clear insight of the spiritual pathway ahead of any individual, thereby encouraging the attainment of personal destiny.

Sand Reading is an ancient art, providing developing sensitives with a positive opportunity to expand their spiritual horizons. As sand is largely com-

posed of quartz, a tray of sand provides a wonder-
fully reflective medium, for it will record the auric
patterns of those who place their hands firmly
upon it.

This then enables those who 'read' the sand to identify, via the colours they perceive, the latent spiritual qualities of the enquirer. Sand reading is something all channels can undertake with a great deal
of success. Objective channels clearly observe the
auric colours impregnated upon the sand whilst
their physical eyes are open but subjective mediums
will need to close their eyes after staring intently at
the sand, in order to 'see' these colourful patterns.

In addition to the auric reflections, there will be
all manner of patterns and images left in the sand
once somone has placed a hand upon it. These
must be translated in a simple and logical manner,
for they have a part to play in the overall communication. With this form of seership, a basic knowledge of the meaning of symbols and colour is essential if the 'reading' is to have any valid meaning
for the recipient.

Flower Clairscentience can be an incredibly accurate
form of seership, one which does not require great
clairvoyant ability. What is necessary, however, is a
basic knowledge of numerology, coupled with an
awareness of the esoteric meaning of colour. (See
pages 100 and 110)

Flower clairscentience should not be confused with
flower clairvoyance, which is a form of mediumship utilising a flower to provide a psychic reading.
This can, of course, prove to be quite meaningful

for the enquirer, but does nonetheless differ quite considerably from flower clairscentience. With flower clairscentience the channel can, by studying every part of the flower, trace a person's 'life-path' from birth onward. In addition they can also identify a particular quality possessed by the person, knowledge of which they glean from the colour of the flower itself.

The first step in this form of channelling is taken by the querant who must select a flower for the 'reading', either picking one of their choice from the garden, or selecting one from a nearby vase, or by purchasing a particular blossom from a florist. Provided that no other person has influenced the selection process, then that flower will provide the medium with a clear insight into the nature of the querant.

Some may dispute this statement, assuming that a flower purchased from a florists or one which has been picked by another person for a floral display, must surely have many vibrations impregnated upon it and that these will therefore influence the outcome of the reading.

That would certainly be a valid point where a medium is demonstrating *flower clairvoyance* . However in this specialised form of 'reading' the channel sets out to interpret the number of leaves the flower has and the various blemishes upon them, whilst noting any damage to the petals of the flower and so on. They must not, at any time, take into consideration any vibrations they may detect upon the flower during the course of this investigation.

The channel studies the flower very carefully. And notes the measure of rigidity in the stem, for this will serve as an indicator of the querant's general responses to outer pressures or stress. Further study of the stem will detect any damage to it and to the leaves, all of which reflect past trauma, and the individuals response to it. The number of leaves appearing at various points along the stem relate to particular undertakings or situations which have arisen in the past, and here the channel does need to use numerology.

Parasites on the underside of the leaves, or petals of the flower, identify a tendency to permit others to drain their energies, whilst water droplets hidden deep within the blossom represent tears which this individual endeavours to hide from the world. Any holes in the leaves or damage to the petals, reveals an inability to overlook past hurts. Details of this nature tend to be overlooked in simple flower clairvoyance, yet have a large part to play in establishing the accuracy of flower clairscentience.

It may not always be possible for the querant to obtain a perfect flower, an overnight storm perhaps destroying the initial choice. However, as nothing happens by chance, the flower presented will carry within its form, colour and blemishes, the information needed at that point in time. Should someone present only the head of a flower or the upper portion thereof, it reflects their reluctance to acknowledge their past, whilst a flowering plant in a pot serves to indicate a basic insecurity, which the individual will need to address.

An **Auragraph** is an ancient Chinese art, whereby

the sensitive charts the patterns observed in the aura being studied. The majority of those who are incarnate on this Plane of Matter have experienced numerous lifetimes prior to their current one. The aura serves to provide a visual record of past attainments.

Elsewhere in this book I have described the nature of the aura and what the various colours therein represent, but that which I now draw your attention to is the outer segment of the aura, that portion which lies beyond the Higher Mental, or Causal Body.

Here the sensitive will observe, in colour and symbol, the qualities of the soul; dormant talents which may be called upon during current life experiences. Some refer to these qualities as 'the gifts of the spirit', yet, as each individual soul has laboured extremely hard (often within the mystery schools of former civilisations) in a bid to develop and perfect these qualities, the term 'gift' is perhaps erroneous. The *spiritual talents* might be a more fitting description.

Light blue identifies a psychic faculty; royal blue and indigo indicate intuitive and clairvoyant capacities and are located in this section of the aura, along with amethyst of the New Age healer and violet which reflects occult knowledge and powers.

In addition, symbolic representations of dormant skills or talents, which need to be reactivated during the current lifetime, will also be noted here. The all-seeing eye indicates the potential for seership. The pyramid represents the necessity to develop a balanced outlook upon life whilst endeavouring to look deep within the self for the knowledge sought.

The channel *must*, at all times bear in mind the fact that all such imagery represents potential - that which is still *dormant* within the querant, and should clearly stress this point when sharing such information with others. Failure to advise any individual that these are qualities of the Soul, upon which they should now focus their attention in a bid to reactivate them, could all too easily propel them toward the pit of spiritual pride.

The role of the seer carries with it a great deal of responsibility, and the onus is upon the channels to translate that which they 'see' in as clear a manner as possible, taking great care to avoid the stimulattion of vanity within those who seek their aid.

Clairvoyance is a quality which differs from channel to channel. Many clairvoyants avoid the use of props, such as a crystal ball or tarot cards, preferring instead to gaze directly at the enquirers, and 'tune in' to their energy for a brief period, before sharing with them that which they 'see' or 'hear'. Once again, the quality of the information obtained in this manner, depends to a great extent, upon the measure of training the channels have received, their level of evolution to date, and whether they endeavour to bypass the Astral Plane in their search for truth.

The great majority of those who operate as clairvoyants today tend to be psychics; well intentioned individuals who provide a much needed form of service.However, no matter how supportive or comforting such communications may be, unless mediums also place emphasis upon the necessity for growth within the enquirer, (whilst indicating just how this might be achieved), they are, in my opinion, simply abusing their spiritual talents.

Such statements do of course arouse the ire of some who feel that actions of this nature infringe upon the rights of the enquirer, particularly if no request for such information has been received. I do not agree, for this overlooks the Greater Law which indicates that *'when the student is ready the teacher appears'*. Provided that you operate in accordance with that law at all times, then those who are led to you for guidance, will receive according to the need of their *Higher Self*.

Where channels elect to take the 'easy option' and are quite content to act as vehicles for a stream of innocuous communciations from the Astral Realm; or where they focus their attention upon that which they perceive to be the emotional or material needs of the enquirers they could, unwittingly perhaps, encourage these individuals to become dependant upon them and their abilities.

True channels will always endeavour to extend themselves on each and every occasion, being determined to accept only those communications which originate upon the higher sub-plane of the Mental Plane or beyond.

Those who question this statement - and there may be many, would be well advised to give careful consideration to the long-term effects of channelling inaccurate or illusionary 'spirit communications'. If such misinformation causes anyone to take an illusionary pathway through life and thereby fail to attain the measure of growth for which they incarnated, then the channel concerned becomes associated with the karma of failure which eventuates.

We all return to this plane of matter - voluntarily or otherwise - in a bid to attain further growth. Where the opportunity for this is blocked due to a dependancy upon illusionary communications, obtained through channels who consciously abuse both their gift and responsibility, then all participants must resolve this matter at some future point in time.

I repeat, the role of the true Seer carries great responsibility and should never be abused. Within the mystery schools of former civilisations, those who embarked upon this path of endeavour, undertook a seven year period of initiation,upon the completion of which, they acquired the symbolic title of 'The Messenger of The Gods'.

Although the mystery schools no longer exist as such and there are but few sensitives today who are prepared to undergo a truly disciplined training in the art of seership, those who do aspire to become a clear channel for the light of truth, must ensure that they act in a responsible manner at all times.

Failure to heed this warning could result in an inability to activate their spiritual senses in a future incarnation - at a time when all of humanity will be expected to utilise their sixth and seventh senses in a bid to communicate with the higher dimensions, on a daily basis.

Trance Channelling has received much publicity in recent years, and is a type of mediumship which tends to attract a deal of public scepticism. This kind of channelling takes various forms. One 'example' is a light 'overshadowing' where the channel speaks in a normal manner, with voice and features unchanged. Few of those present would realise that the 'inspired' words are a form of actual spirit communication.

More commonly demonstrated is a form of channelling where the voice and features of the channel may alter quite dramatically, and during the early stages of development, the channel's breathing may become quite laboured, causing some alarm in those who witness such activity.

Should channels persist in 'performing' in this manner (without attempting to develop a more harmonious interchange between themselves and their spirit communicators) then it may be that the ego has the upper hand, with the mediums quite simply determined to make a lasting impression on their credulous audience.

There is a further form of trance channelling which was much to the fore during the earlier part of this century, where channels elected to temporarily vacate their body and permit a spirit entity to take full control. The drawback with this particular form of channelling lies in the fact that the mediums have no awareness of what has transpired, and are therefore unable to answer the many questions which arise, once they return to the conscious state.

Where channels desire to expand their level of

consciousness, attaining thereby a measure of spiritual growth, then this latter stage of trance control is to be avoided at all costs, for there is little of value to be gained from becoming a vessel for spiritual truth, if one has no awareness of that which has transpired.

Having had many years of personal experience as a trance channel I can state (with some authority) that all who aspire to undertake this particular form of spiritual service, must from the outset, ensure that they retain full conscious control of their mind and body, if they are to avoid possession by astral entities.

A point not readily understood by many who are fascinated by trance mediums, is the fact that the spirit communicators must first access the mind of the channel concerned, drawing upon all knowledge available therein. Where the channel has no awareness of a specific subject, then there may be no disussion upon it, for the conscious mind will reject any input with which it is unfamiliar.

Trance channels must therefore be prepared to study a great many subjects, acquiring thereby a measure of awareness of many beliefs, in order that their spirit communicators may then expand upon specific points of truth.

The act of channelling should be undertaken in a disciplined manner with channels in a state of receptivity, having first meditated, and prepared themselves well in advance of the event. The spirit beings draw close at the appointed time, and begin to communicate telepathically with their chosen channel. These communications are invariably received as thought patterns arising within the mind, and during the initial stages of development, these are often rejected as figments of the imagination.

At other times these telepathic communications may be 'heard' quite distinctly, sounding - more often than not - like the channe'ls own voice, echoing deep within their head. These also tend to be rejected, for the inexperienced channel often lacks awareness of the existence of a Higher Self (or soul), and the Overself, both of which must use the only voice to which they have access - that of their physical represenative.

At the outset of their development novices have great expectations, eagerly awaiting their spirit teachers, convinced that they will shortly hear a loud voice booming in their ear, telling them precisely what to say or do. Sadly most are doomed to early disappointment. However, as they gradually develop their spiritual potential, they will begin to discern whether the communicant is masculine or feminine. The next step of course is to ascertain whether the information received is pure illusion or reality. . .

CHAPTER TEN

SPIRIT GUIDES
AND HELPERS.

The subject of spirit helpers invariably causes a deal
of doubt and confusion in the minds of those who
begin to investigate the unknown and who may
be puzzled as to why in this modern technological
age, we should require the assistance of discarnate
entities. The fact that many of these appear to have
been monks in the past, or have oriental or north
american indian identities, simply adds to their
overall confusion.

Why are spirit guides and helpers necessary? What
role do they play in our lives? Could we not achieve
our life's task without them?

As to why they are necessary, we simply have to
look back to those difficult situations which occur
from time to time when in sheer desperation, we
have called upon God for assistance. Naturally we
anticipate some form of constructive, three dimensional response, but what usually happens, is a
form of inner guidance or 'knowing', which then
enables us to resolve the situation for ourselves.

Assistance of this nature quite often comes from the Doorkeeper, also referred to as the Guardian Angel, whose task it is to guide our steps through material life. This is one of two spirit entities we must all select prior to each period of physical experience.

They are selected from among members of our Group Soul - souls whose level of evolution is similar to our own and with whom we have forged strong links throughout time. The Master Initiate under whom we have studied since time began for us, would have indicated those who have the requisite knowledge and experience, from which we might benefit, during our current sojourn upon the Plane of Matter.

Prior to physical embodiment, we must spend a deal of time with these two special souls, who will guide our steps through the many difficulties that await us during the incarnation ahead. However, once incarnate, memory of the past is erased along with all knowledge of these two non-physical aides. And when they attempt to forewarn us telepathically of the dangers that lie ahead, we tend to turn a deaf ear to their timely words of warning, and are then left to experience a particular situation for ourselves.

When this happens we tend to become indignant that the Doorkeeper failed to 'prevent' the occurence, but as these souls are not permitted to interfere with the expression of our free will, all they can do is to forewarn and then step aside in order that we may absorb the lesson which any given situation has to teach us.

The role of the Doorkeepers is a lengthy one, as

they accompany us upon our journey to the Plane of Matter, and from birth onward, they endeavour to guide our steps throughout our entire life experience, before leading us back once more to the realms of light at the moment of physical death.

The second of our spiritual assistants is known as the Mentor or Spirit Teacher - again an old friend. with whom you will have experienced much in the course of earlier incarnations. Their role usually commences when we reach the mid twenties, at a time when the personality is begining to expand its influence, and the search for meaning within life begins.

The role of the Mentor is an onerous one, for to them falls the task of stimulating awareness of spiritual purpose. Where we are observed to be spiritually weak, then the Mentor will stimulate a desire for a strong religious support group, and guide our steps toward an appropriate belief sytem.

Where on the other hand we are judged to be strong enough spiritually to take responsibility for our own thoughts and actions, we are then lead toward an inner awakening, and the subsequent activation of our spiritual talents.

The Mentor and the Doorkeeper then work together to ensure that all aspects of our life experience; mental, emotional, material and spiritual, receive due attention, enabling us to attain a measure of growth on all levels.

The support we receive from these two beings is constant, despite our tendency to stray from our spiritual path from time to time. They too have faced similar situations in their past, and therefore they will not reject us for our human frailties. The link with these beings is, at all times, one of loving support and spiritual camaraderie

Being non-physical, they may only communicate with us telepathically, and during early childhood they have little difficulty in so doing for, until the soul fully occupies the body at around seven years of age the intuitive and clairvoyant faculties are still active.

From that time onward, the Lower Will fixes its attention upon the attainment of its three dimensional goals, and little or no attention is paid to the Higher Will and its desires. It is only when we reach the age of twenty five 'approximately' that spiritual awareness begins to stir, at the instigation of the Mentor.

Where we have incarnated to fulfil certain spiritual tasks we may, as we awaken spiritually, attract (toward us) other spirit helpers, who are drawn by the light within our aura. These entities could perhaps be termed 'ships that pass in the night', for they owe us no allegiance, and may well seek to aid several spiritually alert individuals at one and the same time.

These spirit beings themselves desire growth, which cannot be readily attained upon their own level of consciousness. Indeed, they may only progress via an act of service to mankind, sharing their knowledge with those who endeavour to expand their spiritual horizons. This in turn serves to trigger awareness of long dormant spiritual talents within those who heed their call. All life-forms are inter-dependant and until we can come to accept this truth, adjusting our thinking accordingly, we cannot achieve any meaningful measure of growth or attainment

The point of attraction lies within our aura, and where this indicates the possession of a latent spiritual quality or talent, those discarnate entities who possess similar skills then draw close, attempting to influence our thinking by directing our attention toward suitable books, or on occasion, teachers who will assist us to activate that talent.

Some among us incarnate with a specific intent, ie: to take giant strides toward spiritual self-mastery, a goal which may only be attained with determined self discipline and a committment to serve mankind. Such individuals attract toward them a number of spirit helpers all eager to play a part in this task.

As to why many of these helpers portray themselves as monks or indians, the answer is really quite simple. The image they project is intended to identify the role they are to play. Where they portray themselves as Chinese, the helper may be signalling their ability to provide spiritual truths, for the ancient Chinese possessed great wisdom. Furthermore, they were extremely well versed in the healing arts, and it is equally possible that such a spirit helper wishes to assist by stimulating awareness of a dormant healing ability

Should helpers manifest as nuns or monks, it is often an indication of their desire to serve in a humble manner, and does not necessarily indicate that they were once within the cloister. However, where they appear as priests or bishops, it clearly identifies a role they played in a former lifetime, and the part they are anxious to play in your life ahead. Quite often the helper who assumes the identity of bishop, is drawn toward those individuals who have incarnated to shepherd others toward spiritual awakening and the attainment of personal destiny.

Those who appear as Aztec Indians, or who identify with former civilisations in Persia, India, or Atlantis, seek to stimulate awareness of an earlier incarnation (and quite possibly) of a time when the individuals concerned were associated with that entity.

Sadly, some misguided people begin to worship their spirit helpers, endowing them with knowledge and powers they do not possess, and quite often, refusing to take any action in a given situation until their 'guide' instructs them accordingly. Indeed, over the years I have encountered a number of seemingly intelligent people, who simply refuse to rise from their beds in the morning until they have received clearcut instructions on the days events from their' spirit guides'.

This of course is sheer folly. The Creator provides us all with the gift of free will, the possession of which sets us apart from all other life-forms on this planet. We should not abandon this to follow the bidding of any other being - spirit or otherwise -

unless we have given the matter much serious consideration. Further, it is an extremely dangerous course of action, for such behaviour can so easily open the way to possession by astral entities and this, in turn, may well result in a lengthy stay in a 'secure institution.'

The Mentor and Doorkeeper, together with the various helpers we attract toward us along the way, may only *guide* or *direct* us. They may *not* interfere with our free will, which is our God - given right. Where we foolishly surrender this to an astral entity, who may claim to be a highly evolved soul, then we are failing to utilise our powers of discernment, and must expect to pay a high price as the result

When assistance of any kind is required, we should always direct our thoughts, prayers, etc. to The Father / Mother God, and we will be answered according to need. In such situations we must of course also bear in mind the desire of our Overself, which may wish us to undergo a measure of difficulty or suffering, in order that it may learn from our responses to such situations.

We are all interdependant and none among us may attain their personal destiny unaided. The assistance rendered by our unseen spirit helpers is therefore invaluable and should be duly appreciated as such. Nonetheless, they are but the representatives of The Creator, drawn to our side in our hour of need.

Provided that, at all times, we retain a true perspective of the role of the spirit helpers are intended to play in our lives, all will be well.

CHAPTER ELEVEN

THE POWER
OF
THOUGHT

In acting as channels for communications from the
non-physical dimensions, intuitive and clairvoyant
mediums become receiving stations for the
thought processes of those discarnate beings, who
dwell on the higher planes of consciousness.

Telepathy - or thought transference, is their only
means of communicating with mankind, and before venturing into the field of spirit communication, the aspiring channel would be well advised to
acquire a full awareness of the incredible power of
thought.

By and large we tend to be creatures of habit and
quite often the habits we develop are detrimental to
our wellbeing. And yet knowledge of this fact is
rarely sufficient to dissuade us from self-destructive
practices. This is certainly true of our daily thought
output, with few among us stopping to ponder the
effect such thought patterns have upon our lives.

Whenever we release emotionally charged thought

patterns into the ethers they have much the same effect as throwing a stone into a pool; the ripples they create extend far and wide affecting others in the process. What is more, the consequences of such acts will serve to influence our lives in a manner we can scarcely imagine.

When we indulge in negative thinking, such as worrying over the health of a loved one or fearing the onset of an unwanted situation, the matter does not end there. The 'offspring' or 'out-picturing' of our mental processes begins to take form in the ethers, and will return to cause havoc in our lives. The very situation that we so worried about, takes shape before our eyes.

On every level thought brings influence to bear. In our own lives and in the lives of others. Where we worry constantly over a loved one or friend, we are surrounding that person with a negative thought form. Persistent worry re-energises the thought form. For example, many mothers feel that unless they 'worry' about their children they are not 'good' mothers. . . Eventually this will result in negative activity taking place around the person we love.

Why, and how, this occurs, is due to the involvement of the Lords of Form. These ethereal beings, take the energy released by mankind into the ethers as thought power, and fashion from it a corresponding counterpart or thought-form.This then remains in the ethers until its creator (you/me) is ready to deal with it. Should we continue to re-energise that thought form by further negative thinking, it becomes more and more potent.

Fortunately, not all of our thought output is so destructive, and those loving or caring thoughts which we also send out daily result in constructive situations. This is the reason why prayer, sent out on behalf of others, is so very effective at times. Where we pray long and hard, for the resolution of a difficulty that a friend is experiencing, those caring thoughts may result in a positive outcome (as we would see it) - provided that it is to the long-term benefit of the person concerned.

This latter statement may puzzle some, but we must always bear in mind the outworking of the Natural Law, or the Law of Karma. We may well wish to see an end to the suffering a friend endures but where that suffering reflects a measure of cleansing (or karma) then our prayers may appear to have been fruitless. Yet on a higher level, those loving and caring thoughts will serve to strengthen our friend, and give courage to endure that which lies ahead.

The power of thought can, of course, be used by determined individuals to attack others, although the subsequent repayment (karma) for such activity is not something I would wish to experience. Activity of this kind is often sparked by that most destructive of all human emotions, jealousy. Here I refer to the practice which is termed 'psychic attack' a most unpleasant experience from the point of view of the recipient, whereby they are constantly attacked by repellent thought forms

Such attacks usually occur when people are most

vulnerable - during the sleep state. They awaken to find a horrendous form, which is neither animal nor human, approaching their bed. Speaking from personal experience, the initial reaction is one of sheer terror, an automatic response which unfortunately, serves only to strengthen the intensity of the thought form. Although it is quite natural to fear such attacks, the energy from this emotion then renders the victim helpless and, in due course, the sender of the thought form gains the ascendancy.

Many methods are recommended for warding off such attacks, although I have doubts as to the efficacy of placing a clove of garlic in the bedroom! As the majority of psychic attacks are experienced in the region of the Sacral Chakra, or the navel, the wearing of a tumbled piece of Carnelian in the navel overnight, does indeed serve to ward-off such attacks.

However, when seeking to counter attacks of this nature, the only true remedy is the use of a counter-thought pattern, taking care not sink to the level of the attacker. The method I suggest is extremely simple, and importantly, is one which breaches no spiritual law, therefore it will not bring retribution upon the head of those who utilise or follow it.

This method involves the Law of Forgiveness, which is *the* spiritual law,coupled with the Natural Law (See chapter 8). When under attack, endeavour to set aside any animosity or fear, and send out a thought of *'unconditional love '*, or visualise a ray of Rose Pink light, directing this toward the attacker (where their identity is known).

Maintain this for several minutes before adding
'I forgive you . . .' Finally, call upon the Supreme
Being,"Father/ Mother God, I ask you to transmute
this negativity which is not of me, and return it to
its source." Where you are unaware of the identity
of your attacker simply focus your mind upon 'the
source unknown. . .'

The fact that you are unable to identify the source of
the unpleasantness makes little difference to the
outcome, provided your response is sincere. In this
manner the Natural Law (karma) is blended with
the greater Law of Forgiveness, (which brings
about redemption). From the blending of these two
great laws comes the Law of Initiation. Therefore,
out of this unpleasant but cleansing situation comes
growth.

The attacker meanwhile, must take on board their
own thought patterns duly transmuted into light.
For them, the net result can be most unpleasant for
such individuals are, more often than not, under
the influence of dark forces. This unexpected inrush
of unconditional love coupled with their own light-
charged thought forms, will be most unwelcome
and impossible to repel.

The clearest example of the Law of Forgiveness in
action, was that given by Jesus of Nazareth, as He
hung upon the cross..."Father forgive them, for they
know not what they do".

Always bear in mind the fact that thoughts have life
once they are released by the mind, and therefore
have the power to influence our future, together

with the future of others. The role of the Seer must also embrace that of the Teacher and those among you who truly desire to become The Messenger Of The Gods once more, must be prepared to instruct those who are drawn to you by the light in your aura.

CHAPTER TWELVE

REINCARNATION

Any book which deals with the art of seership should contain any information pertinent to it, and there is one subject which many channels find unpalatable. The belief in reincarnation. The majority of mediums accept that the spirit-self survives physical death, continuing its existence upon another dimension. Whilst they will happily communicate with those discarnate entities, when the subject of reincarnation is raised, it is often dismissed out of hand.

I am constantly amazed at this response. If the spirit - self survives, then surely it is logical to expect a return to the world of matter at some future point in time. So let me push back the frontiers of your mind and, together, let us ponder this most contentious subject.

Each life experience has a particular pattern, an individual destiny, which the soul has incarnated to attain. The Soul is the reincarnating entity, a timeless being which has set out upon this journey into matter once more, in its progress towards perfection.

With each successive incarnation, the soul adopts a whole new persona. All knowledge of past is erased, together with any awareness of the overall purpose for the current life experience. In this manner, the soul is provided with a great many opportunities to respond in a positive manner, to situations which may have defeated it during previous incarnations. And so growth is achieved.

By and large, the majority of opinion falls into one of two camps. Those who accept reincarnation as a logical part of the process of evolution, and those who simply reject the concept out of hand. It is difficult to blend a belief in the Christian teaching of the forgiveness of sin with the immutable law - karma. What is more, after three score years and ten few among us relish the prospect of yet another period of experience upon this Plane of Matter.

Throughout time great minds have taught that not only do we appear many times but that we must return again and again, until a state of perfection is reached. The Lord Gautama (Buddha) stated that the only form of spiritual democracy which can exist in space is the privilege of each individual to perfect themselves.

Plato accepted the fact that the soul was immortal, and declared that it was imprisoned in the body, like an oyster in a shell. He regarded the physical dimension as a sphere of retribution - the real hell if you wish - and taught that reincarnation was essential to the ultimate perfection of our divine nature.

Pythagorus also taught reincarnation and stated that the soul, passing through the cycle of necessity, experienced many different personalities at different periods of time. He had memory of many of his former incarnations, and often spoke of them. As Euphorbus he was wounded in the battle of Troy by Menelaus, the husband of Helen.

In his next incarnation as Hermotimus he saw in the temple of Apollo a shield which appeared familiar. Subsequent enquiries revealed that this shield had been donated to the temple by Menelaus, follow ing that famous battle. According to Heraclitus, Pythagorus also stated that in an earlier lifetime he was the Herald, Aethalides, who was reputed to be the son of Mercury.

Many Christians dismiss the subject of reincarnation claiming that the Bible does not refer to it, yet in Matthew XV11, verses 11 to 13, Jesus does in fact allude to it, when he asks His disciples "Who is it that they say that I am? Is it not that I am Elias who was to come? Yet when Elias came they knew him not." Then the disciples knew that he spoke to them of the Baptist.

Within the mystical orders of the Christian faith, the concept of reincarnation has always been seen as a natural part of our evolution, a point brought home to me some years ago in England, when I was asked by the Churches Fellowship for Psychical Research to give a talk on the aura. Before being permitted to speak, I was taken into a side room and questioned very thoroughly on my subject. Eventually the subject of reincarnation was raised, and I was then told the following story.

"A young man had decided to enter a monastery.

Together with his father, he spent many hours trying to choose a name suitable for his new vocation, before finally selecting the name of John. (which means 'of God', or 'God is gracious'). On the day of his induction, as he was led away to commence his new life, his father spoke proudly to the abbot, telling him of the time they had spent in selecting his son's new name.

In reply, the abbot said "His name will be Stephen", (a name which means 'Crowned One'), and turned away. This response quite incensed the father of the novitiate who replied angrily, "Surely my son has the right to choose which name he will use for his new vocation!" The abbot turned, smiled and then said, "That was his name before; it shall be his name once again."

The abbot was providing a clear indication, that he was aware that this young man was about to repeat an earlier life experience, and would therefore be given the same name, possibly in a bid to test his reactions to the energies this would now introduce into his life.

Reincarnation and the Law of Nature, go hand in hand.This great law is also known as Cause and Effect, or Sequence and Consequence, or again, Karma. This law binds all life-forms together. Not simply mankind, but Man with the Animal Kingdom too. Together we comprise one huge family with an inseperable, although complex history. This is one reason why humans should not mistreat animals.

The quality which sets humanity apart from all other life forms is that of free will - the ability to choose - a

Divine gift which we all abuse at some point during our evolution. As a result, we incur debts, or karma, which must be balanced at some point in time. If this concept can be grasped and accepted, then it can change your whole outlook on life. Any activity which causes loss or suffering to another must at some point in time be resolved by undergoing cerain unpleasant personal experiences.

Karma is not always an unpleasant experience, for in our past we have all taken time to care for or to assist those less fortunate than ourselves, rarely seeking or expecting any reward. Yet the Law of Compensation is very just and, at some future point in time, possibly during another incarnation, there will be chance encounters with apparent strangers who purposefully seek to assist us during times of difficulty.

I have lost count of the wonderful situations which have come into my life through the intervention of total strangers (as I have travelled from country to country over the years.) Whenever I have been beset by difficulties - in themselves the outworking of this great law - these familiar strangers have appeared on my path, and have brought good fortune in their wake.

When first encountering the Law of Compensation (karma) many puzzle over how such a law functions, given the size of the world population. How could every act, positive or negative, be noted and recorded, with due repayment being exacted ?

This task falls to the Lords of Karma, of whom there are four in our solar system. They are specifically

concerned with the evolution of the human race,
and theirs is the duty of noting all that transpires
on the Plane of Matter. A task of this nature requires a great deal of assistance, and co-operating
with them in this work are many initiates and
devas.

Jesus of Nazareth spoke indirectly of the role played
by these Great Ones when He said that "Not a bird
in the sky falls to the earth without my Father in
heaven knowing of it." The Lords of Karma are the
Planetary Mediators and the Keepers of The Akashic Records - also known as The Book Of Life.

In addition to repaying a measure of our personal
karma (see chapter 8) we are also expected to repay
a portion of the karma accumulated by the various
groups with which we become associated. To us
therefore, falls a measure of Family Karma, coupled
with a portion of Racial Karma. Furthermore, we
must play our part in resolving National Karma,
and World Karma. When we have resolved our
part in National Karma, we often migrate to
another land, and there must assume our part of
the karma associated with that nation.

As the Lord Buddha once said, "Effect follows cause,
as the wheel of the cart follows the oxen." Rebirth
into matter takes the place of faith and atonement,
providing each soul with the opportunity to master
self and overcome personal weaknesses.

The true seer will, from time to time, be provided
with knowledge of, or receive visions appertaining
to an earlier life experience of those who seek their

assistance. Such information is often provided in a bid to stimulate those concerned, into action on a particular level, and seers who block their mind to truth of this nature, rob those who search for truth.

CHAPTER THIRTEEN

ASTRAL TRAVEL

Many people today are greatly fascinated by astral travel, with some spending many years - and a great deal of money - learning how to project themselves consciously from their physical body into the astral realm. That this can be achieved is not doubted, for a number of Indian yogis have written on this subject.

After all, we all leave our physcal form during the sleep state and journey to other planes of consciousness. Although few among us return with memory of these astral journeys, it is within the realm of possibility to retain awareness of our nightly journeys. However, it does require a deal of determination and perseverence.

Before I deal with how this might be achieved, let me first explain just what is meant by the term 'astral travel'. Elsewhere in this book I have described the subtle bodies, and it is to the second of these, the Emotional or Astral Body that I would direct your attention. (See page 106)

The spirit-self (being pure energy) does not require to rest, as does its physical counterpart. Therefore, as we sink into the sleep state, the Emotional or Astral Form detaches from the physical, and moves out into the Astral Plane, which interpenetrates our world of matter.

We may experience this as a sense of floating away from, or hovering above the body - which in fact is what is taking place. At that point most people then fall into a deep sleep, and have no further awareness of their astral journeys.

At times, we may experience a sensation of falling from a great height. This occurrence is usually experienced immediately prior to waking, often just as the alarm sounds. It can occur shortly after dropping off to sleep. Experiences such as this, indicate a very rapid return to the physical body from the astral realm. Often, this is accompanied by a feeling of terror; a wildly beating heart; and a sense that something unpleasant has happened. In situations like this, we tend to put on the light in order to reassure ourselves that all is well, and soon sink back into sleep.

Experiences of this nature usually arise, following encounters on the lower astral plane. It is here we locate those entities who, whilst in the physical form, were totally self-focussed and downright unpleasant. As part of our spiritual growth we must all volunteer to visit these dark planes during the sleep state, in a bid to encourage those who dwell thereon to move toward the light. As light is something they fear they tend to attack the light bearer, who then retreats very swiftly to the safety of the physical form - with a wildly beating heart.

If we were to stop at this point, and endeavour to reactivate memory of what had preceeded the sudden return, it is quite possible that full awareness of the experience would re-surface. But, in the majority of cases, the sensation of fear associated with it is sufficient to cause most people to block out the memory.

Our Higher Self does endeavour to make us aware that we have spent time out of the body. To this end it will often cause us to have strange ' waking dreams,' such as having traversed exceedingly long buses or trains and, just as we reach the last car, the alarm will sound.

At other times we may remember descending very swiftly down an enormously long ladder prior to waking. Or of being balanced upon a single, rocket propelled roller skate and awakening at our appointed time.

Retaining memory of astral travels can be achieved in one of two ways, both of which are attested to be successful. The simplest of these lies in utilising a small cloudy or opaque quartz crystal and programming this to achieve the desired goal.

A cloudy crystal has a relaxing (feminine) energy, whilst the clear quartz will stimulate activity - both mental and physical - and is hardly conducive to restful sleep. Therefore, for this purpose, the cloudy quartz should always be used.

To program the crystal, first cleanse it in a solution

made from one teaspoonful of sea salt (*never sea water*) and one teaspoonful of apple cider vinegar, placed in a small bowl containing a cupful of warm water. Immerse the crystal in the solution for ten minutes to cleanse it of all chemical residue and of any emotional imprint left by other individuals, who will also have handled it.

Rinse the crystal in cold water and then, holding it in the *left* hand, position it just below the base of the throat, and begin to project a thought pattern of '*love* ' toward the elemental intelligence, which has its being within the crystal. Gradually a stream of cool, tingling energy, will begin to flow from the crystal into the region of the throat, which is the signal that the elemental intelligence is responding to your loving input.

Now, mentally project the instruction "record all dream state activity. " and place the crystal beneath the pillow. From that point on no other person should touch the crystal for if they do, their emotional imprint will eradicate your program. Just as you settle down to sleep take hold of the crystal and reactivate the program, first by directing '*love*' to the intelligence, and then saying "from this moment on record all dream state activity. . ."

Should you awaken during the night or early in the morning, with a vague memory of a wonderful experience; which tends to vanish as soon as the conscious mind becomes involved - take out the crystal and command it to "replay dream state activity. . ." The crystal will then stimulate awareness of that night's experiences.

I must emphasise here, that the crystal is acting as a link between the subconscious mind (which has full awareness of the journey) and the conscious mind (which does not). The information is not retained by the crystal. If you do not then write down the information received, it will be lost.

This practice does attract a deal of scepticism, which is a perfectly natural response. But if quartz crystals can be utilised in similar ways in the many electronic devices we now utilise, why not in this manner? Many people dismiss my suggestions as arrant nonsense. Yet, when they do act upon them, discover that they do indeed, prove to be an effective manner of recording astral travels. (My earlier work Crystal Healing, provides much more information on the use of crystals.)

The second method of retaining memory of astral journeys lies in instructing the mind, prior to going to sleep, "I will return with memory of my astral journey...". When first awaking, endeavour to activate conscious awareness of the experiences of the previous night, knowledge of which is lodged in the subconscious memory. This method is much more laborious; requiring a great deal of patience, but it does pay dividends, in the long term.

Just what is the Astral Plane? What transpires there that is so important to us? The seven sub-planes of the astral form a non-physical dimension which, nonetheless possesses a degree of materiality. It is to this plane of consciousness that we all go, when we die.

Should you wish to link-up with someone who has passed to the higher life then, prior to going to sleep issue a mental instruction to this effect to your Higher Self, adding that you also wish to return with full memory of that encounter. Quite often, you awaken with memory of a dream, in which you did encounter your loved one.

Upon the various sub-planes of the astral, we may all travel forward in the continuum that we call time. Time of course, is an illusion; for past, present and future are all in the now. This is why some mediums are able to predict the future, and others may perceive the past. On the Astral Plane, we may also, from time to time, experience events that lie before us, situations we are to undergo in the physical body several days ahead.

When this occurs we find ourselves in familiar surroundings and know in advance just what is about to take place, or what is to be said, and by whom. By and large, these uncanny experiences are dismissed by the majority, as mere imagination, or classed as inexplicable, few ever stopping to ponder upon them, or to ascertain just why everything appears so familiar.

Some incorrectly assume that the sense of familiarity is due to their having visited those areas, or encountered those individuals during an earlier incarnation. But usually, the answer lies in nightly encounters upon the astral planes. Those who wish to utilise their nightly journeys to gather knowledge, may do so by requesting, prior to slumber, that they be permitted to visit the Halls of Learning; and that they will subsequently return with full memory of whatever has been absorbed there.

Finally, many people have 'out of the body' experiences which, again, are intended to trigger awareness of a Higher Self. There are many recorded instances of individuals who have undergone the death experience and came back. Most claim to have gone foward into a brilliant light which was warm and welcoming but, eventually, were told that they must return to the physical dimension.

I know of one lady who, although interested in spiritual matters, had great difficulty in accepting that her life had any real purpose, or that her soul, if she possessed one - would return to matter at some future point in time. Yet, following a major operation to replace a hip joint she was bewildered to find herself hovering above her body as it was wheeled from the operating theatre. This experience taught her that there were two seperate aspects of her self and this stimulated her to seek for greater awareness.

This world of matter is a vast illusion, and not the reality it may appear to be. This we shall all discover in the fulness of time when we move on to other dimensions, (each of which will appear to be as real and as solid as our present dimension). Where we are seriously searching for truth, and desire to acquaint ourselves with other planes of consciousness, then we will indeed return with memory of our 'out-of-the-body' experiences.

Sufficient to say, that we have all incarnated once again in a bid to further expand our level of consciousness and to achieve a greater measure of growth, which may only be acquired through the experience of the many challenges we encounter on this Plane of Matter. Let us not waste this valuable opportunity by constantly endeavouring to escape from our physical form, for in so doing, we merely exchange one form of illusion for another.

CHAPTER FOURTEEN

SURVIVAL
OF THE SPIRIT

Survival of the spirit has always been extremely logical to me having, throughout my childhood, clear memories of my earlier incarnations in Atlantis. (Some of which I recount in my earlier book, Vision Tomorrow.) Such knowledge does not necessarily make acceptance of a future role any easier and, although I am of Celtic origin - a race renowned for its *fey* qualities - members of my immediate family, tend to feel uncomfortable in my presence. .

I am not the first in the family to demonstrate such uncanny abilities. Indeed close relatives were extremely psychic, particularly the sister of my maternal grandmother. Those aunts who could be persuaded to speak of her did so reluctantly, for she had been a fairly well known psychic in the north of England, during the early part of this century.

An uncle was psychic during his childhood according to my mother, but he determinedly blocked this ability in his late teens. My mother was also very mediumistic although in her later years, she became very fearful of the unknown. This I found most surprising for Mother had acted as the channel for Wen Shu (my spirit mentor) when he desired to instruct me during my early childhood. My sister was always sent out to play on such occasions, whilst I had to sit and listen to the lesson for the day - much to my annoyance.

In the years leading up to her death, Mother would often comment. "I do wish you would keep your spirits to yourself. . ." One day, tired of simply ignoring these comments I asked her "what on earth do you mean?" Relieved to be getting some response on the matter Mother then told me that she would regularly awaken in the night, to find a group of spirit entities gathered around her bed. "And they must have been looking for you. . ." she added in an admixture of fear and humour.

As we lived some sixty miles apart that was highly unlikely but I could not convince Mother that my helpers knew exactly how and where to locate me and, therefore, any entities gathered around her bed were those who wished to be of assistance to her.

The passing of my mother was quite an educational experience; humorous in retrospect, but difficult to deal with at the time. I would like to share this tale with you for it provides a wonderful confirmation of the survival of the spirit.

Prior to her death my mother suffered greatly with a very painful form of cancer. She underwent the accepted form of treatment for this condition, and slowly began to regain weight appearing to me to be on the mend. As the result I decided to go away for a week to the Findhorn Community, situated in the far north of Scotland. Much to my regret, I failed to advise my family of my destination; a thoughtless act which had some long-term repercussions.

During my week in the Community my whole outlook on life altered, and I became aware of the need for the total dedication of the self to a greater cause. It was whilst I was in the midst of this stage of transformation, that my mother attempted to make contact with me. I could hear a woman's voice calling out my name but, try as I might, I could not locate its source and so, finally, I dismissed the matter from my mind.

During the course of that week - one which embraced the Autumnal Equinox - my clairvoyant faculties expanded and I left at week's end in a state of some confusion to make a long train and bus journey to my home on the south coast of England. Bleary eyed from lack of sleep I arrived home to discover my mother awaiting my return - and a telegram on the mat. I had little need of the telegram for I could see quite clearly that mother had made the transition but, as I was soon to discover, she was not fully aware of the fact.

She began to question me at length on where I had been etc, and finally I had to tell her that she was no longer in the physical form. "Dead! What ever do you mean? Dead? I am standing here talking to you. I am not dead - and what is more, I have no intention of dying. . ." Eventually I begged her to allow me to lie down and go to sleep. "Then,' I told her, "I will be in the spirit body, and we can talk for as long as you wish." This appeared to placate her, and she allowed me to go off to sleep.

My rest was shortlived. Within three hours she had me fully awake, telling me that she wanted to go out once more to see the coastal town I lived in. Also to say goodbye to someone that she knew. This I found heartening for it indicated that she had begun to accept her new environment. I was soon to be dissuaded of that.

I trekked down to the sea front and at her insistence walked along its full length before wearily turning for home. However, mother insisted insisted that I take a longer route home, one which took me past the home of one of my students with whom she had formed a friendship. As we passed the gate of this house mother stopped. Lo and behold, the front door opened and out came my student clad only in her nightdress.

I was quite astonished, and said to mother "How on earth did you manage that?" but got no response. I then had to tell her friend of Mother's death,which is possibly the reason she had engineered this situation. During the following week Mother made a thorough nuisance of herself, forever telling me that I should clean my home (ignoring the fact that I had been away), that the curtains needed cleaning, the windows required washing, etc.

The funeral was held that weekend at her home in Kent to which all of the surviving members of her family came. On the morning of the funeral the funeral Mother was quite excited, for it was some years since she had seen all of them together. By this time Mother had learned to communicate with me at will and obviously assumed that she could now talk to anyone as she wished. On this point she was soon to be dis-illusioned.

All of mother's sisters were gathered outside the bathroom and mother endeavoured to make her presence known to each of them in turn but with no success. Eventually , she came to me in quite a distressed state. "They will not speak to me" she wailed."But of course not" I replied. " They cannot see or hear you." "But you can - why can't they?" she continued tearfully. I tried hard not to smile. "But you know I have always been a little odd and, besides, whilst you were alive you were not too keen on talking to spirits either." She made no further comment but stayed with me quite dejected.

Later in the morning the wreaths began to arrive. As there were so many of them they were all placed on the lawn in front of the house. Mother told me that she wished to go and look at them. As we stopped to look at the various tributes she paused to pass comment. "Oooh! just look at that beautiful one, and that one... I never thought that she would send me a wreath."

In the midst of this inspection the elder of my two sisters joined me. She was deeply distraught at our Mother's death, and I feel a little puzzled as to why I showed no grief. As she tended to be more afraid of my beliefs than Mother had been, there was little I could say to comfort her. I was now faced with the task of continuing a conversation with Mother, determined to inspect all of the tributes, whilst also talking with my sister.

Naturally I very quickly ran into trouble for as I muttered answers to Mother my sister looked at me most oddly. "What did you say?" she asked. "Oh nothing." I replied. "Yes you did" she responded, " you said something about that wreath. . ." This conversation was cut short by the arrival of the hearse which triggered an emotional response from Mother.

Her own mother had died some six years earlier, and since that time there had been some conflict within the family over the care of the grave. This had distressed mother considerably and she had left quite explicit instructions as to what was to happen to her body after death. She wished to be cremated - and that moment had come.

Although Mother had accepted - in part - her new dimension she still related to the earth and, what is more, she still identified with her earthly form. So far as she was concerned her physical body was all that she knew, and it was now time for this to be cremated. She was terrified.

As the pallbearers stepped from the car, wearing enormously high top hats, she grabbed hold of me and cried out, "Eeeh! I'm not going in the fire. . . I'm not going in the fire. . ." Momentarily forgetting my sister, who by now was in tears, I said to Mother, "It is alright. . . you don't have to go into the fire. Just stay with me". My sister stared at me uncomprehendingly through her tears: "What do you mean? What are you saying?"

I was saved at this point by the family filing out to take their places in the cortege. I sat beside my sister, whilst Mother sat on my knee, clinging to me fearfully. At the crematorium, Mother stood right by my side quite determined that she would not enter the flames.

Then a most amazing event took place. The coffin, (covered in floral tributes), lay before the curtained entrance to the furnace. Suddenly, five spirit beings appeared. Four of them taking up positions at each end of the coffin, slowly walked forward. The fifth entity - a North American Indian - came toward Mother, offering her a long violet robe trimmed with gold. This she accepted without question.

An ethereal version of the coffin now emerged, on which were laid wreaths that were twice the size of their physical counterparts and from which a deal of light flowed. Without further ado, Mother went off quite happily with the entity who had handed her the robe. I appeared to be the only person who noted these amazing events and the service continued, with none about me any the wiser.

I was nonplussed. What did it all mean? Why were the flowers upon the spirit coffin larger and brighter than those in the physcial tributes? Wen Shu was soon by my side to answer my questions. He told me that the robe was my Mother's spirit robe, and that it's colour and pattern served to identify her level of spiritual evolution. The light emanating from the flowers on the spirit version of the coffin, he said reflected the love which came from their physical counterparts.

That was not the end of the days events, for Mother turned up at the wake, insisting that I tell the entire family what had transpired that day. This was a rather difficult request as the majority of the family held decided points of view with regard to my beliefs. As Mother kept insisting I eventually plucked up my courage and told them everything which had happened that day and during the week previous.

My story was met with a stoney silence. All avoided my eyes, their grief and confusion quite apparent. Then one of my aunts - the wife of mother's psychic brother, came up and threw her arms about me, thanking for me sharing the experience. "You have helped me to accept death," she said through her tears. (Some years later I was to assist her again, following the death of her husband.)

I did not see my mother again for some months, then one day, in the midst of a healing session, I noticed her in the corner of the room, observing what was taking place. A little surprised, I mentally enquired if she had come to assist, but she shook her head saying "No, I have just come to watch." Some two months later she re-appeared, having made her transition. Gone was the astral body. All I could see was my mother's face surrounded by many points of light, as though she were wearing a diadem of light. She smiled at me and vanished.

It took some thirteen years for my mother to free herself from the astral planes and during that time

I had no contact at all, apart from an occasional encounter on the astral during the sleep state. Then one day a figure, clad in a hooded white robe, appeared at my side whilst I was in the midst of my accounts.

The hood was pushed back and there was the familiar face of my Mother. I was quite taken aback, and my only response was "And why are you wearing that robe. Have you joined the white brotherhood?" This I said rather caustically, but her rejoinder was gentle, if reproving. "This is how you will see me from now on. I have finally found my true self." With that she vanished, but from time to time, I am aware of a figure in a hooded white robe by my side who never speaks.

Two other expriences are worthy of sharing for they serve to show how the thought patterns and beliefs we maintain throughout life tend to create an illusionary world beyond the Plane of Matter.

My aunt - mother's youngest sister, died some four years later, also from a painful cancer. There was not much difference in our ages, and we had always been very close throughout my childhood. Her husband had loved her deeply, and had her body embalmed, keeping this in the family home for a week prior to the funeral.

Some three months later I was visiting Australia, where I endeavoured to complete my book Vision Tomorrow. In the midst of this task I was surprised to see this aunt appear before me, in a very distressed condition. Laying aside my manuscript, I asked what it was that she wanted. "Eeeh Edmund! just look at what is happening to me" she cried, showing me that whilst half of her body appeared intact, the remainder had turned black.

I then had to spend a considerable period of time patiently instructing her on how to detach from her now decaying physical form and encouraging her to accept that her true reality was the spirit-self. This was not an easy task and continued over several nights largely on the Astral Plane.

The story had a sequel some two years later, when I visited her daughter in the north of England. I told her of my experience with her mother and she stared at me in amazement. Although more accepting of my beliefs than the majority of the family, she was still, nonetheless, fearful of the unknown.

"That explains it!" she said, half in wonderment. "Explains what?" I enquired."Well," she responded "for about three months after mother died, whenever all of the family met at Dad's home, we would all smell the embalming fluid. No one could explain why. It did not occur unless all of the family were there. Then after three months, it suddenly ceased."

Quite obviously my aunt, being earthbound at that time, tried to establish contact with her loved ones by introducing the smell of the embalming fluid. It was only after my intervention that this ceased. Not having a belief in an after life, being embalmed only encouraged her to assume that her body was now preserved for ever, although just how she related to life in limbo I do not know.

The final experience relates to my mother's psychic brother. Although he was a man who called a spade a spade, he never passed any comment, in my hearing at least - with regard to my clairvoyant abilities. I must also say that he did not discuss his own ability in this field either.

A year or so before his death, one of his legs turned gangrenous and had to be amputated. He took this very hard. The day after I learned of his death I was hanging curtains in the bedroom when I heard my uncle's distinct Geordie accent. "Ah've got me leg back now ye nah! Tell wor Mabel that ah've got me leg back..". Then he vanished.

Passing this information on to his wife was far from easy for she was surrounded by a number of extremely protective daughters most of whom had not encountered me in the flesh. When finally she did come to the phone, I told her, as gently as I could what her late husband wished her to know. There was a very long silence before I received any response. "Thank you Edmund for taking the trouble to ring me. I do appreciate it." and she hung up.

Whilst recalling these incidents from my past and endeavouring to complete this manuscript by a particular date, my labours were repeatedly interupted by a series of spirit encounters. The final outcome of these 'ghostly' experiences was of such a meaningful nature that I want to share them with you, highlighting as they do a major obstacle to progress upon the non-physical Planes of Consciousness.

Once the soul has undergone the 'death' experience

there are certain things it undertakes almost immediately. The primary task is to review all the activities of the recently completed lifetime. During this review the soul takes note of situations where it may have hurt or injured others - whether due to thoughtlessness, or its own calculated responses to the actions of another.

As each event is reviewed the now disembodied spirit entity not only observes the effects of past actions upon all concerned but, in addition, must also experience these from the point of view of the recipient. Reviews of this nature are often extremely unpleasant. Unfortunately this experience alone is insufficient to erase the matter from the Akashic Record (or the Book of Life).

The soul may then attempt to correct past actions by seeking the forgiveness of all those who were involved. This requires the assistance of an intuitive or clairvoyant medium. Those who fail - for whatever reason - to follow such a course of action, must remain upon the lower sub - planes of the astral, caught up in their own emotional thought forms. Such events could be likened to that which some faiths refer to as purgatory or even hell depending upon the nature of past actions.

Now to the events which have triggered this additional information. I learned that a very dear friend had suffered a stroke shortly after celebrating her eightieth birthday. In response I commenced absent healing - directing healing thoughts toward her. A week or so later as I sought to complete my manuscript, I became aware of the presence of a spirit entity.

As it has long been my practice to refuse to accept those communications which originate upon the Astral Plane I determinedly ignored the entity. Eventually the intensely cold psychic force, which identifies such entities, became too much to bear and I finally capitulated, acknowledging the presence.

"Hello!" I called out. No response. "Look, I am pretty busy at the moment so please do me a favour and just go away... " I was not able to identify my ghostly visitor due to my tendency to 'see' in a subjective manner - ie with my eyes closed. The entity ignored my request, drew even closer. The psychic vibration now became intense and was quite unbearable.

"Oh! Alright - I give in. What is it that you want?" Once again there was no reply. I tried for some considerable time to elicit some form of response all to no avail, so in frustration I returned to my labours. (I must state here that my mind was firmly fixed upon completing this manuscript by days end and this played a large part in my inability to communicate with my visitor.)

Throughout that day and for part of the night my unwanted guest remained close by my side, the presence clearly identified by the intensely cold vibration. Becoming irritated by all of this unwanted attention I finally called upon the spirit helpers associated with the entity to come and lead them to their rightful Plane of Consciousness.

This plea was soon answered. An elderly Chinese male helper clad in black silk appeared, and as I sent out thoughts of unconditional love and light toward the entity, they were slowly lead away. The change in the room's temperature was almost instantaneous. However, the relief was to be shortlived for within fifteen minutes my visitor had returned.

It was not until the following morning that I caught a brief glimpse of the entity. "Joan!" I cried in total astonishment, for until that moment I was unaware that my dear friend had passed to the higher life. She smiled briefly giving me a slow handclap before disappearing. That evening her son phoned from England to tell me of the death of his mother some two days earlier.

The next day my friendly spook was back again but as before, there was a distinct lack of communication. "Joan!" I cried out in desperation."If you have something to tell me please do so, or at least try to send me a mental image that I can translate. But do not simply stand there - your vibration is difficult to bear." Alas my plea went unanswered. It took the remainder of that day to discover the reason for my friends visit - she wished my forgiveness for something which had occurred some fourteen years earlier.

I was quite astounded. "But Joan I forgave you for that many years ago and we resumed our friendship. I bear you no illwill whatsoever." Her joy at my response was quite tangible before she slowly faded from view. However, next morning, she returned. (I had by this time abandoned any hope of completing my manuscript by the appointed date for every time I sat at the computer Joan would appear).

She was now becoming adept at communicating. "What is it that you wish to tell me this time?" I asked. There was silence at first and then hesitantly she asked me to contact her daughter. "Caroline?" I cried. "No Joan I am sorry, I refuse to telephone your daughter. We both know her opinion of mediumship etc." Many years earlier I had attempted to instruct her daughter together with a group of her school friends on esoteric matters, but the experiment was a failure and Caroline was now a respected academic.

Joan was deeply upset and refused to go until I finally agreed to ring her daughter the following day. As the week progressed Joan expanded her new-found ability to communicate telepathically. Day after day she would ask me to intercede on her behalf, ringing a number of friends whose forgiveness was vital to her further progression.

Once the funeral had taken place the visits ceased for a day or two and when she did return, it was to offer me healing for a troublesome health condition. Our communications were still of a telepathic nature which I found to be somewhat frustrating. As the weeks passed Joan began to bring former associates - known to us both - who had also passed over, each one wishing to say a final farewell.

One day Joan began to project a mental image gradually revealing to me the light of her aura. This was a major step forward and since that time she has developed her ability to communicate in this manner. In a remarkably short time she has shown me how she has adapted to her new environment - having left the Astral Planes behind her and resumed her true identity once more. In addition she has begun to reveal aspects of a former life we spent together, fragments of which I had uncovered many years ago.

This for me was a major learning experience as I came to a full realisation of just how potent our thought patterns are and how those charged by malice, anger, or jealousy, fashion a web we cannot escape in the after life. In order to free the self some attempt at atonement has to be made.

The seer must always be prepared to become a teacher, although it is well nigh impossible to become a prophet in one's own land. To this end I have shared some of my personal experiences in these pages in the hope that many may learn from them.

CHAPTER FIFTEEN

EARTH-BOUND ENTITIES

Talk of the survival of the spirit following physical death invariably leads to discussion of earthbound entities; ghosts and poltergeists as they are more commonly known. Few among us care to accept the existence of such entities, indeed most assume that tales of ghostly beings are the product of an over-active imagination. Yet throughout time, tales of haunted houses have been shared with great relish. You must ask yourselves, "Is there more to this than a mere collection of hair-raising stories, created to while away idle hours. Do such entities exist? "

Speaking from personal experience I can attest to the veracity of these tales, having had many visitations from earth-bound entities when visiting the various towns and cities in the many countries in which I have lectured in over the years. Unfortunately, these entities do have the unnerving tendency of making their presence known in the wee small hours - at a time when one has sunk into a deep slumber.

This results in fear, leading to the temptation to flee

the environment for ever more, although such actions are rarely practicable. Despite this I, myself, have fled one such house in the early hours of the morning, so great was my fear at that time.

Just what are ghosts and why do they haunt certain buildings, some for hundreds of years? The answer lies in the life that entities live whilst still in the physical form, their belief system and, often, the manner of their death. Thought is a potent force, and the thought patterns we indulge in during our earthly lives, tend to fashion the next stage of experience, one we must all undergo following physical death.

A soul can become trapped upon the lower astral plane due to a lifetime of adherance to a very narrow belief system. When they pass from the physical body at the moment of death they have great expectations that they will now be gathered up to sit upon the right hand of God. When this does not occur these souls become greatly confused. An experience in New Zealand some years ago best illustrates this point.

Sitting at breakfast with my hostess prior to my morning meditation, I finally plucked up the courage to ask her why she had banged upon my wall for so long in the early hours of the morning. As I have a tendency to snore, I felt certain that she was about to complain about this habit. However, she was quite mystified at my question, telling me that she had not done so.

Deciding to leave well alone, I changed the subject,

yet over the next three days, and always just before dawn, the banging would awaken me. Now I fell to wondering if, in fact, it was the tenants in the nearby apartment who were being disturbed by my snoring. Deciding that I needed to clear the matter up I again spoke to my hostess, who assured me that no-one had complained to her, and that she had heard no-one banging upon the wall. As this house was constructed largely of wood I was even more puzzled.

As we talked I became aware of a spirit entity standing beside my hostess. When I mentally enquired who it was she duly told me her name. This information I then passed on to my somewhat astonished friend, who finally replied, "Oh! That is my mother - she died three months ago. Whatever does she want?"

The entity then became very distressed, and kept repeating... "Jesus never came...Jesus never came..." What happened then was quite puzzling for me. A man appeared, dressed as a pastor and holding a bible. He began to thunder at the unfortunate entity, telling her that she must desist, that she had no right to tell me this..." As I relayed this information to my incredulous friend, the entities disappeared. I then asked if any of this made sense to her.

She was somewhat nonplussed, "That was not my mother at all, but my aunt. She was also called Eadie. They were sisters-in-law." She was greatly intrigued by what I had told her for her aunt had passed over a year earlier, but they had never been really close. She explained that the man I saw had indeed been a 'hell-fire and brimstone' pastor in a very narow and rigid christian sect, the woman being his daughter.

Apparently, he had dominated her entire life and she had willingly given up all thought of a personal life. Having been taught to love none but Jesus she deliberately shut out all forms of loving expression and lived strictly in accordance with the tenents of her faith in the full expectation that, in return, Jesus would come to collect her when she died. So strong was her tie to her father that she had insisted that her body was to be buried on top of his when she passed away.

However, the early-morning knocking on the wall continued and at breakfast some days later the aunt returned, still deeply distressed. Once again, she told me "Jesus never came . . ." Her niece and I surrounded her with unconditional love, but this appeared to distress her all the more. Eventually I was shown an image of this woman sitting all alone in a park.

I was then told that this unfortunate soul would have to remain in virtual isolation on the lower Astral Plane until she had learned to respond to love, something she had deliberately refused to do throughout her life. After sharing this information with her niece I asked her if she would be willing to spend a little time each day surrounding this lost soul with unconditional love, which she happily agreed to do.

You may ask why this soul was apparently being punished when, to all intents and purposes, she had lived a very moral, and thoroughly christian life. However, love is all. It is the source of life itself. In living so strictly in accordance with a dogma that ran counter to all which the Master Jesus had taught, this being had apparently cut herself off from Him. It is not my intention to pass a moral judgement in this situation. I am merely reporting what transpired.

Do bear in mind the fact that this soul had spent more than a year of earth time on the lower Astral Plane pondering her predicament. In finally establishing contact with her niece in this desperate manner, she took her first hesitant steps toward freedom.

This tale did not end there. The early morning knocking continued day after day, all of which I now tried to ignore, having placed Aunt Eadie in the care of her niece. Then one evening, as I sat discussing spiritual matters with a visitor, my hostess fell asleep in the chair opposite.

Our discussion was rudely interrupted by the sound of someone knocking loudly on the front door, which was on the lower floor. The noise awakened my hostess who sleepily went to see who was at the door. To her surprise, she discovered no one there.

Rather puzzled, she began to climb the stairs but the knocking recommenced, this time from a point on the upper floor. I now joined in the search for its source but neither she nor I could trace its cause. Until that moment my hostess had not heard the

knocking which awakened me daily and so we fell
to discussing the matter with our visitor, arriving
at the conclusion that it must be her aunt endeavouring to communicate once more. Our guest turned very pale."You are surely not trying to tell me
that the noise we heard was made by a ghost - are
you?" he stammered."Oh yes" I replied quite cheer-
fully "they regularly bang on the wall here." With
that he took his leave and fled into the night.

Our nocturnal visitor was not to be dismissed so
easily and very soon made its presence known to
me. This time it was indeed the mother of my host-
tess, who, it soon transpired, was also caught up
on the Astral Plane due to action she had taken
many years earlier at the suggestion of medical
authorities, with regard to the welfare of her youngest son. The emotional conflicts arising from this
unjust act and the need to ensure a measure of justice for him in a particular situation prevented this
soul from moving on to her rightful place in the
higher ethers.

The double task of seeing to her brother's wellbeing,
and praying for her late mother in a bid to free her
from an emotional void fell to my hostess. My role
in these matters then came to an end. Both situations do, however, clearly identify just how our
everyday thought patterns, and subsequent actions,
serve to tie the soul to the outer reaches of the
earthplane, following physical death. It was only
the determination of both souls to establish contact
with me, that brought about a resolution of their
predicaments.

This story does not, of course, fit too easily with the usual ghost tale, for the souls concerned were stuck on the astral, and were not tied to the physical dimension. The following experience however, does fit the classic pattern, and was for me, quite a hair-raising one.

This occurred in the late 1960's at a time when I consciously endeavoured to reactivate the clairvoyant ability I had so determinedly blocked, during adolescence. I was visiting a friend in North London, who shared a large and very delipidated Victorian house with several other people. As the owner of this building had recently passed away, they decided to accomodate me for the night in his former quarters on the ground floor.

It was a stormy evening and during the course of dinner, I became aware of a spirit entity standing beside me. At first I endeavoured to ignore her, but the intensity of the cold, psychic energy with which she manifested made me blurt out to my friend - a dour and extremely sceptical Scot - "There is a woman here, and she wants to talk to someone."

There was a deathly hush, broken by my friends curt "Shut up Edmund."He glared at me, and we continued with the meal. However this old lady was not about to be dismissed and drew even closer. I made several attempts to draw the attention of the group to this entity, but each time my comments were cut short by my short-tempered friend, and as the remainder of the party were beginning to look very nervous , I abandoned the task, telling the entity to go away.

When I finally retired for the night, I found myself in a rather grim, and extremely dirty room, piled high with the dead man's possessions with a single bed made up in the far corner.There were two locks on the door, a mortice and a yale, so I locked both although one would have been sufficient. It was bitterly cold in this room, and the storm outside seemed to be increasing in its intensity. Torrential rain lashed against the illfitting windows, which shook and rattled in a wind that howled like a banshee. I swiftly dived under the covers and fell asleep.

An hour or so later I was awakened from a deep slumber, by the sound of a door constantly banging in the wind. I did my utmost to ignore this but whenever I dozed off, I would soon be reawakened by the noise. I lay there hoping and praying that soon someone on the upper levels would go and close whichever door it was but, alas, my prayers went unanswered.

Eventually, when I could stand it no more, I put on the light, to discover that it was my door which was banging to and fro. Greatly puzzled, for I was certain that I had locked it prior to going to bed, I firmly closed the door once more, ensuring that both locks were in place before returning to bed. Within ten minutes the banging had recommenced, this time much louder than before.

Now the hair on the back of my neck began to stand on end. The door was swinging to and fro; the temperature in the room appeared to have dropped considerably, and I had to face the fact that some one was trying to communicate with me. Terrified,

I sat up in that darkened room and asked "Who is there?" The answer was swift. The elderly woman I had encountered earlier in the evening now stood by my bed. "What are you doing in my house?" she asked angrily. I tried to point out that she was dead and that the house no longer belonged to her.

"Dead? I'm not dead! What are you doing in my house?" she repeated angrily. I then tried another approach "This is 1969, when did you live here?" I asked. This puzzled her for a moment. "No it isnt, its 1944, and there's a war on." It slowly dawned on me that this woman must have been killed in a bombing raid, and was still tied to the environment with which she was familiar. As she refused to heed what I said, I called, in desperation, on my spirit mentor,Wen Shu who, together with her own spirit helper finally led her away.

It eventually transpired that this soul was so earth-bound that she rejected all offers of assistance from the spirit side of life, unable to relate to the non-physical dimension. As all else had failed, I was utilised in a bid to establish current earth time, and her present state of being. This situation often occurs where souls do not believe in an after-life or where their belief has taught them that they must wait for the day when the last trumpet sounds

This latter belief was obviously the reason why a young Italian girl still slept many centuries after her death, sometime during the 16th century. It was a rather bizzare experience which occurred during a stay in a small pension on the Isle of Capri.

Once again I was awakened in the dead of night, by a loud banging on the underside of the iron bedstead, with which my tiny room was furnished. An unknown voice repeatedly called out "Maria. . . Maria. . ." I was not too impressed by this activity and simply went back to sleep.

The knocking continued however, now louder than before, whilst a male voice continued to cry out "Maria. . .Maria. . .Maria. . . " Blearily awake by now, and more than a little irate, I responded "I do not know anyone called Maria", but just as I was about to drift off to sleep once more, I suddenly remembered that I did have an aunt Mary.

Sitting bolt upright in bed I discovered, to my great surprise, that the walls of my small room had vanished, and there before me lay a rather beautiful glass coffin, about which was coiled a serpent, fashioned from brass. In the coffin lay a very attractive young girl about seventeen years of age who had long dark hair to her waist. Her clothing was medieval in appearance and in her clasped hands was a single red rose. The voice continued to call out call "Maria. . . Maria. . ." but she slumbered on.

I then realised that I was being asked to try to awaken this soul from an eternal sleep but, alas, I could not make any impression upon her and had to admit to failure. Finally, after some time the voice and the vision simply faded away. I have often pondered upon this experience, for it illustrates just how a religious belief can keep a soul in limbo.

A more recent experience certainly fits the pattern

of long-time haunted houses and, for me, it was quite unnerving. I was lecturing in England and was invited to stage a two day workshop in a stately home in Lincolnshire. Upon arrival I was taken to my room, which was very large, with little more than a double bed at one end and a wardrobe and basin at the other. As I was extremely tired from travelling, I lay down to rest.

The moment my eyes closed I felt fingers tugging at my hair. Sitting bolt upright I gazed around, but I was the sole occupant. Dismissing the experience as imagination I lay down once more, but no sooner had I done so, than the tugging at my hair recommenced. I tried brushing the unseen hands away, but they continued to tug. As I was so weary I decided to ignore my ghostly visitor, soon dozing off to sleep.

Some fifteen minutes later I was awakened by the sound of drums. Not one drum, but a great many, as though there were a miltary band playing outside the house. This I found more than a little puzzling as the manor was some considerable distance from the nearest small town. The drummers played on and when I awoke an hour later, I could still hear them.

As I needed to press my suit before the workshop the following day, I went in search of the lady of the manor, an old friend, asking where I could find an ironing board etc. She was a little nonplussed at first. "Well, I have not seen one of those for years, but I suppose there must be one. Let's go and look in the laundry. " With that we set off into another part of this rambling house.

Opening a door into a dark, narrow passage way, she led me into a large, dimly lit room, which was dominated by a huge contraption in an enormous glass case. This strange apparatus was connected by wires to a nearby bed and looked for all the world as if it were a prop from some horror movie. "What on earth is that" I enquired, never having seen its like before. "Oh", replied my hostess, "that is a marvelous machine. Lie on the bed and I will give you a demonstration." I backed away. "No thanks. Some other time perhaps" I repled hastily. "Where is the laundry?" She hurried ahead. "This way" she cried, leading me into a small room.

There was a deal of light here, with the late afternoon sun streaming through the windows. "Now where is the iron?," she asked aloud, rumaging through the shelves. "Oh! here it is - and look, there is an ironing board" she said pointing into a corner. "I haven't used these for years, so I hope that you know how to operate them." Leaving me to my task she withdrew, and I began to press my suit, my mind upon the strange events that had taken place.

My musings were interrupted by something I observed out of the corner of my eye. I put down the iron and stared into the dark room beyond. My blood turned cold. There was a tall dark figure clad in the oddest of clothes, wearing a high, rounded hat, in which was stuck a long black feather. But it was the total absence of light which struck me the most, as though this were but a black shadow(or shade) and not a thing of substance at all.

This apparation certainly did not wish to be observed for it was on tiptoe, stealthily creeping away,
and then just as suddenly, it disappeared into the
wall. I was momentarily terrified, for I had never
witnessed anything of this nature before. Although
clairvoyant, I tend to observe the non-physical dimension with my eyes closed, and any spirit entities I
encounter, tend to be radiant beings. This spectre
however was quite the reverse and, what was more
alarming, in order to gain access to the main area
of the house, I would have to pass through the
room beyond.

Returning to my ironing, I swiftly completed my
task, with one eye on the room ahead, wondering
what on earth I was going to do next. Grabbing my
suit, I ran through that darkened room as swiftly
as I could, and bumped into my hostess in the hall
outside. "Whatever is wrong?" she asked, noting
my ashen face. When I told her what had transpired, she burst out laughing.

"Yes", she cried, wiping away the tears of mirth, "he
can startle you. At times, he will simply walk right
through you as you enter that room." Quite shaken
by what had occurred I followed her into another
part of the house, where I then shared my experience with those of my students who were gathered
there. I realised much later that I was being deliberately tested by my friend, who obviously wished
to ascertain if I were truly clairvoyant.

I learned later that the entity I had encountered was
the ghost of an ancestor who had been killed in the
house whilst hiding from Cromwell's forces. Centuries later he was still trying to escape, tragically

trapped in a time warp, unable to see or to relate to the present occupants of his former home forever trying to escape his ultimate end. He was not, as I discover later, the only lost soul in that house.

I noticed something rather odd about this grand old house. Nailed above every door and window there were stars, fashioned from a base metal. Unable to contain my curiosity, I asked what purpose they served. My hostess, who now felt that she could be totally honest with me, told me that they were placed there as a form of protection; for when she had first arrived at the house as a young bride, she found the non-physical inhabitants to be quite hostile. Apparently the energy of these symbols served to reduce, although not totally overcome, the negativity of the ghostly inhabitants.

I then asked her why the band had played outside the house during the afternoon. There was a deep silence before she responded "What band? We have no band here." I was puzzled. "But there was" I intjected. "In fact it was most odd, it appeared to be composed only of drummers." At this comment she burst out laughing. Puzzled I waited for an answer.

"The room you are sleeping in was once my late father-in-law's bedroom, and for some years he was a drum major in the army." My heart almost stopped beating for a while as I remembered the fingers tugging at my hair and the fact that I was to spend two nights in that room. "But why is he earthbound?" I asked.

She then told me that he had been a heavy drinker, and unknown to his family, had squandered the family fortune on women prior to his death. When this was discovered, his wife cursed him - and there he stays, seeking to gain attention in whatever manner he can - and which he continued to do for the remainder of my stay. Sufficient to say that a restful night was hard to come by in that house.

Later that evening, I encountered yet another of the long-term residents; the ghost of Lady Chaplin, who was born in the house and died there at the age of 101, without ever really leaving it, and what was more with no intention of doing so now.This entity I found to be the most difficult to handle, for she resented intruders, and sought to make their stay as unpleasant as possible.

I was not alone in encountering unexpected occupants, for there appeared to be one in every room of this great house. Many of those who were participating in the workshop (dealing with the development of mediumship), had also been invited to stay, and some were doubling up, sharing rooms. The shrieks of terror which rent the night, as fearful young women discovered ghostly intruders in their rooms, made certain that this was a weekend to be remembered by all.

I did endeavour to ascertain from my spirit inspirers the reason for the level of ghostly actvity in this house, and whether the souls trapped there could not be released. Eventually, I learned that in part, the measure of activity was due to the level of the Ley Energy (or earth power), traversing the area the house was built upon. I was also told that the entities were not aware of each other, trapped as they were in their own concept of time, but were fully aware of those they considered to be intruders, in other words, the present day inhabitants.

Strangely enough, they did not trouble the present owner, a descendant of the family who, centuries before, had built this house on the ruins of a much older building. It was as though they recognised his right to be there. As to being rescued, the entities showed no interest in being freed from their time-warp, and had to be left until they desired to move on.

With all of the situations I have described, and they are but a few of those I have experienced, those who were earthbound could not accept the fact of physical death and, having no concept of a higher life, they therefore remained attached to that which was familiar. Any changes made by later occupants are never noticed, they perceive things as they were, and new occupants as intruders to be ousted - hence the hauntings.

I have shared these experiences in order that the awakening sensitive may become aware that such entities do exist and that, wherever possible, the medium should endeavour to assist these unfortunate souls to move on. However, do be prepared for disappointment for, over the years, I have found that although they may wish to communicate, most entities show a marked reluctance to move on, and such activity can prove to be quite unnerving, if not downright unpleasant.

BIBLIOGRAPHY

Throughout my life, I have come across certain books which have triggered powerful responses within me, each in turn casting light upon my spiritual pathway. I list some of these below, in the hope that others will seek them out, and gain as much from them as I have done.

Alder, Vera Stanley. The Finding Of The Third Eye. Rider, London 1938
Dawkins, Peter/Trevelyan Sir George. The Pattern of Initiation.Francis
                              Bacon Research Trust. Northampton 1981
Hall, Manly P. Reincarnation. .Philosophical Research Soc. .Los Angeles
                                                                    1971
Hall, Manly P. Sages and Seers. Philospohical Research Soc. Los Angeles
                                                                    1959
Heindel, Max. The Rosicrucian Cosmo-Conception. Fowler, London 1909
Powell, A.E. The Astral Body. Theosophical Publishing, London 1927
Powell, A.E. The Causal Body. Theosophical Publishing. .London 1928
Powell, A.E. The Etheric Double. Theosophical Publishing. London 1925
Powell, A.E. The Mental Body. Theosophical Publishing, London 1927
Rolfe, Mona, Initiation By The Nile. N.Spearman, London 1976.
Rolfe, Mona. Spiral of Life. N.Spearman, London 1975
Rolfe, Mona. Symbols For Eternity. N.Spearman, London 1980
Randall-Stevens, W. Book of Truth. Knights Templars of Aquarius.
                                                       London 1976.

Vision Tomorrow

In an enthralling narrative Edmund Harold takes the reader through past, present and future scenarios, revealing through his clairvoyant faculty images of cataclysmic earth changes to come.

Closely in line with predictions from sources as diverse as Astronomy and Geophysics, one must pay heed to the ever increasing body of informed opinion warning of difficult times ahead in man's history.

Edmund Harold's prognosis is in essence an optimistic one. If we will heed the warnings in time, we have it in our power to influence the course of events.

Originally published in 1981, a number of the situations forseen by Edmund Harold have now come to pass or are currently under way as the world and the human race undergo ever more challenging situations.

An exciting book on many levels.

Recommended Price $14.95 (Australia)

Available from your esoteric book stockist or direct from the publishers, Grail Publications, P. O. Box 2316, Port Macquarrie, NSW 2444.

Master Your Vibration

Numerology is an ancient science, one which is gaining wider acceptance day by day. The priests of ancient civilisations coupled this with its sister science of astrology in a bid to provide those who sought their aid, with a clear overview of their purpose in life.

On a day to day basis, each and every one of us is subject to certain subtle energies, these in turn influence our thinking process and emotional responses. The ancients identified these energies with numbers - each having a positive and a negative vibration. Human nature being what it is, we tend to take the line of least resistance - and therefore often fail in our life's task.

Edmund Harold casts new light upon this subject, providing all with an insight into just how we may, with determination, expand our level of consciousness and tap into the wisdom of the Hierarchy.

Inspired by the Master R., Edmund gained insight into just how those who do endeavour to reflect the positive aspect of their numeric patterns, may in turn receive inspiration from particular Ascended Masters.

A thought provoking book .

(A new edition will be released by Grail Publications in mid 1995.)

CRYSTAL HEALING

It is becoming more and more apparent that the humble quartz crystal has extraordinary properties. It can help heal the sick and improve the energies, concentration, decisiveness, empathetic qualities and state of balance of the healthy.

This 'modern' discovery is really a resurfacing of ancient knowledge, and, while the knowledge and use of quartz crystal power has had a continuous history ever since its ancient origins, it is now entering a renaissance. Much of what was lost is being slowly pieced together anew.

In *Crystal Healing* Edmund Harold addresses in particular the healing power of crystals, through discussion of the characteristics of the different types of crystals, how to select crystals and how to use them to achieve harmony of body and spirit.

Available from your local book store.

KNOW YOURSELF, HEAL YOURSELF

We all need a restoration of body and spirit at certain times in our lives, but how can we achieve it? Internationally known healer and lecturer Edmund Harold has brought together in this book information about a wide range of therapies that includes crystal healing, therapeutic touch (a kind of hands-on balancing technique), numerology, colour healing, music therapy, resonance therapy and astrology.

Know Yourself, Heal Yourself is invaluable for both lay person and healer: it will help those who wish to have a greater understanding of themselves (body, mind and spirit) and why they react to certain situations or conditions in a particular way: and it will direct those who wish to practice the art of healing.

As well as setting out clearly the philosophy behind each of the healing practices it describes, the book explores the practical aspects of working with people and 'energies'. Edmund Harold provides detailed descriptions of the various areas of the body involved in healing, such as the endocrine system, the chakras and the organ meridians. He gives numerous real-life examples from his thirty years experience in the field of natural healing therapy, and many practical approaches to healing such as visualisation and guided imagery, meditation and crystal balancing.

Know Yourself is essential reading for all those who wish to explore health and healing in its many aspects and for healers and aspiring practitioners.

Available from your local bookstore.